PAUL HOGAN

The Real-Life Crocodile Dundee

Sandra Jobson

W H ALLEN · LONDON
1988

First published in the United States of America by
St Martin's Press, New York, 1987

Set in Baskerville by Phoenix Photosetting
Printed and bound in Great Britain by
Mackays of Chatham Ltd, Chatham, Kent
for the Publishers, W.H. Allen & Co. Plc
44 Hill Street, London W1X 8LB

ISBN 0 491 03456 3

Oz Wizard

'G'DAY! – MICK DUNDEE – I'm from Australia.' With a cheeky grin and a firm handshake, a new superstar is born: Paul Hogan, the blue-eyed, blond, unlikely sex symbol from the Land Down Under, whose film *Crocodile Dundee* has rocketed into the realm of the all-time movie greats, elbowing aside such blockbusters as *ET*, *Star Wars*, *Rambo* and *Top Gun* in box office takings.

When I was asked to write this book I was delighted to do so, despite the lack of first-hand material available. It's always nice to write about someone you like and admire. It's about time more people knew more about this likeable man's rise to stardom – particularly in America and Great Britain where the public have taken him to their hearts. Fans deserve to know more about their heroes – and Hogan's story is a remarkable one. Perhaps Paul will tell his own story someday. It will be something further to look forward to. Sifting through all the information – and misinformation – that has been written about him, I have tried to sort out the fact from the fiction. Sometimes this was impossible to do completely. Paul Hogan protects his private life zealously.

Essentially this is the story of a 'little Aussie battler' who, with his comic genius, down-to-earth personality and rugged good looks, won through against odds that most people would have found daunting. For 30 years Hogan drifted through life, finding doors closed against him, yet convinced he was destined for better things. 'A Cinderella in hobnail boots' is how he describes himself as he bounded from one low-wage job to another. Yet even he, in his wildest imaginings, never thought that one day he would be the number one Sex Symbol in the USA and be invited to open the 59th Academy Awards ceremony in Hollywood in front of Tinseltown's greatest stars, plus 100 million television viewers around the world. And all because of a film – a 'feel-good movie' as he calls it – about a crocodile poacher from the Australian Outback who, with the help of a pretty girl, makes it to what he calls 'The Big Smoke' and triumphs over its evils and pretensions.

For non-Australian readers, a glossary at the back of the book will help guide you through the maze of slang which constitutes the language of 'OZ' – as Australians affectionately call their country. Words marked with an asterisk (*) will be found in the glossary.

Given that most of the Paul Hogan story comes from published sources, it is right that I thank the staff at the following libraries: Australian Consolidated Press; Fairfax Magazines; the *Sydney Morning Herald*; News Ltd; Newsweek (USA); the UK Press Association and the British Film Institute. My thanks, too, to the New South Wales Department of Main Roads. I would also like to thank all those journalists, who, like myself, have met and interviewed Paul Hogan and have provided glimpses into his life. Finally, I would particularly like to thank Mairin Smith,

Lesa Tinker, and Madelaine Morel for their invaluable assistance.

SANDRA JOBSON, 1987.

CHAPTER 1

G'day!

LIGHTS . . . CAMERAS . . . ACTION! The scene is Hollywood. The date is 30 March 1987. The occasion: the movie world's Big Day of the Year, the Academy Awards ceremony, the night, as the publicists say, the industry pays homage to its own. And as the night of a thousand stars begins, the TV cameras focus in on a trim, tanned figure immaculately clad in a white tuxedo. It is Paul Hogan, star of *Crocodile Dundee* and recently voted one of the world's most watchable men.

'Hello, viewers,' he begins. Then he offers some sage advice to the winners. Not to put too fine a point on it, Paul Hogan slayed them in the aisles with his quick quips and easy insouciance. He jokingly gave the nominees Hogan's tips on how to behave as they went up on stage to receive their Oscars. 'Firstly, winners,' he said in his slow Aussie drawl, 'when you make a speech it's a good tip to remember the three G's – be gracious, be grateful, get off. And secondly, winners, don't be too humble tonight because we have the second envelope, so don't get up on stage and say "I don't deserve this award". If you feel you really don't deserve the award just give us a wave from your seat and we'll open the second envelope and give it to someone else.'

He also told the nominees that if they didn't have a speech prepared they could see him backstage as he had a 'heap' of ready-made speeches for every category. Holding up one, he read: 'I'd like to thank my mama, my papa and the good Lord above. . . . Sorry, that was for the country music awards!' He had some advice for the nominees who didn't win: 'Let's not have a spectacle of all four losers – I mean non-winners – giving that smile that says: "I'm glad he won instead of me." Think of the TV audiences and give us a bit of variety. If you can burst into tears, that'd be good. Storming out of the building in a huff would be nice, and what's wrong with a nice bit of old-fashioned booing?'

Mentioning that he himself had been nominated for Best Original Screenplay, Paul said he realized he wasn't the hot favourite. 'But I came 13,000 miles for this – I came from the other side of the planet – and if they read out someone else's name instead of mine it's not going to be pretty.' The award went, in fact, to Woody Allen for *Hannah and Her Sisters*. Paul exhorted the guests to keep up the electric atmosphere right through the long ceremony: 'As a television show it does tend to go slightly off the boil, particularly towards the third and fourth hour. So fellow workers, brothers, stay in a sweat and remember this programme is live and there are about one thousand million people watching YOU.'

The live audience, which included Liz Taylor, Bette Davis and Jane Fonda, cheered him to the rafters. Hogan had won himself a few more million fans. His suave performance in front of his movie peers proved how wrong Carl Reiner, MC at a 'roast' earlier in the day, was when he said, introducing Paul, that what made the Australian star so special was that 'this guy has no apparent talent whatsoever.' Reiner was closer to the mark, though, when he added, 'But he is charming.' There's no doubt that Paul is indeed charming. But it took much more than mere charm for this man of humble origins to stand on that dais, before that august collection of stars, and introduce the Academy Awards. The appeal and the success of Paul Hogan is a fascinating phenomenon.

To start with, he's the only 47-year-old sex symbol who looks 47 and gets away with it. His eyes are even bluer than Paul Newman's, and the blond hair on his chest makes sophisticated women go weak at the knees. Wherever he goes in the States, he's mobbed by female fans desperate to say more than 'G'day' to this handsome hunk from the Outback. Yet on the bare face of it, if you hadn't ever seen Paul Hogan and experienced that charm and had heard only that he was a 47-year-old Australian former blue-collar labourer, married to the same woman for virtually 29 years, father of five – and a grandfather – whose hobbies include mowing his lawn, you'd wonder how on earth he ended up starring in a movie that was to become one of the most successful films ever made. And a film that's clean and wholesome, too, featuring only one chaste kiss throughout the entire action. Paul himself professes to be puzzled by how something like *Crocodile Dundee* could turn him into a sex symbol. He says he never set out to be a sex symbol, it just 'kind of crept up on him'. He set out to be a comedian, and though he was always handsome and possessed a superb physique, he never conceived of himself as the matinee-idol type with teenage girls younger than his daughter writing him letters that are so suggestive he's embarrassed to read them. And women of all ages and nationalities calling him 'cute' and inviting him to slip a shrimp on their barbie – anytime.

'Sex symbol is an awful tag in Australia,' he says. 'It means you pose a lot and try to look smouldering and that sort of nonsense. I don't want to be a Mel Gibson type. People with good looks tend to find it difficult to get work when they're 60 or 70. I didn't set out to be a sex symbol – they're from *Young Doctors* (an Australian soap opera) and they disappear in about three weeks. I just wanted to be funny.' Scratching his head, he goes on to say that maybe it has something to do with his age: 'I'm grown up and there aren't too many men over there (Hollywood). They're mostly pretty boys – perfect teeth, square jaws, too much hair. They're all burned out at 40. Or they have mental problems or they've ruined their brains with cocaine or something.' Then he grins and adds: 'The truth is they're desperately short of masculine 40-year-olds. They're looking for a reasonably roughish head. That's OK so long as I cop it sweet.' His co-star in *Crocodile Dundee*, the beautiful Linda Kozlowski, recalled how she reacted when she first saw Paul as Mick Dundee swagger into the outback pub carrying a stuffed crocodile: 'If I could find a guy like that in real life, hell I'd marry him in a minute.'

There is no doubt that Paul Hogan is, as they say, the flavour of the moment. He only missed by a couple of votes the Hollywood Golden Apple award given by the Hollywood Women's Press Club. Up for the award as the most newsworthy newcomer of 1986, he lost out to hunk of the month Mark Harmon. But insiders at the club, which was set up by Hollywood's queen of gossip, Hedda Hopper, confided that Paul Hogan only missed winning because he was unable to be present at the prize-giving, having been tied up in London on business, while Harmon was available. It didn't worry Paul at all, and anyway, when the American magazine *People* put him on its cover as one of the 25 most intriguing people of 1986, Harmon didn't even score a mention. In 1987 that arbiter of US fashion and society, *W* magazine, tiring of Australia being 'IN', nevertheless put Paul Hogan on the top of its 'IN' list – along with Liz Taylor and Richard Nixon. (As *W* itself says, you aren't IN if you take their list too seriously). Today Hogan is now better-known than any of Australia's other Hollywood stars such as Bryan Brown or Mel Gibson. Only that earlier Australian legend, Errol Flynn, comes, as the Aussies say, 'within coo-ee'.* But Paul is catching even Flynn up fast.

In California sex counsellors are advising their male patients to go and see *Crocodile Dundee* to learn how to handle women. Paul is on record as saying that the world has a lesson or two to learn from Australian men on how to treat their women. Reporting from Los Angeles, Australian journalist Jenny Cullen quoted Paul: 'Australian men are chauvinist but as any smart woman knows, that allows *her* to rule the world.' He then gave an example of a woman driving along a road when her car gets a flat tyre. 'What does she do? She gets out of the car and goes yoo-hoo and a man comes along and says "I'll fix it for you" and the stupid man gets dirty and skin off his knuckles and he fixes it up while she stands there and smokes a cigarette and then she says "I couldn't have done it without you" and he beams, feels great, and goes "Yooooo",' Paul said, beating his chest, Tarzan-style. That, he summed up, is how the system works: 'The women have the brains and the men have the brawn.' He added, 'Australian men realized long ago that women were a superior race and we copped it sweet, we do what they want us to do.'

How do you explain the phenomenon of Paul Hogan? What is the clue to his rise to superstardom – probably the only film star whose face was famous first in a series of TV ads before he ever hit the big screen? One answer is that there is something innately appealing in his wholesome masculinity.

Like Jimmy Stewart, Paul Hogan is the quintessential country-born innocent who comes to the Big Smoke and isn't corrupted, continuing to be a real gentleman with homespun charm.

As he grappled with a deadly crocodile in an Outback billabong, saving his scantily-clad co-star in the early scenes of *Crocodile Dundee*, movie audiences all over the world warmed to his bravery, humour and simple manliness. When he landed in the Manhattan concrete jungle, still wearing his battered stockman's hat with snakeskin band, jaunty feather, crocodile-teeth necklace and villainous knife tucked into his belt, the audiences seemed to derive vicarious pleasure from the way this seeming innocent abroad tamed the muggers, drug-pushers and pimps of New York with the same kind of ingenuous confidence that he used to stop rampaging wild bulls dead in their tracks out in the Northern Territory of Australia.

In Mick J. 'Crocodile' Dundee, Paul Hogan has created not just a movie legend but a larger-than-life example of a mythical hero which millions of people everywhere – including suburban Australia – dream of being: the frontiersman who has licked his tough environment by a mixture of muscle and guile.

And there's a great deal of truth in this myth, or rather legend. The great Australian Outback – millions of square miles of dry, hot desert fringed to the far north by crocodile-infested mangrove swamps – is indeed one of the last frontiers on earth. It's hard for people who haven't visited Australia to realize that it is a continent roughly the size of the USA, but with only 15 million inhabitants, most of them living in cities around the coastline. Up north and in the Outback there really are characters like Mick Dundee, out there illegally poaching crocodiles, dynamiting fish, shooting kangaroos, rounding up cattle and herding them thousands of miles, drinking in ramshackle pubs where often the tables are rivetted into the concrete floor to prevent them being thrown in brawls, and sleeping rough around campfires under the stars.

Still, it is curious that Paul's film could compete in audience appeal with such blockbusters as *Star Wars* and *ET*. Mick Dundee didn't have to go into outer space to prove he was a man, nor did he have to be a cute alien to be loved. Above all, he made people laugh. And Paul didn't just star in the movie – he wrote much of the script as well. He puts the success of this relatively low budget (US$6.5 million) film down to the fact that he judged the public right. 'I was fed up with blow-your-head-off movies and figured other people might be too,' he explains. He also felt that it was time a movie was made for women to laugh at. 'Women are always the best laughers,' he says. When he was planning the film he set himself little rules about what not to put in it: 'I wouldn't have 48 cars smashing into each other for a cheap laugh. I wouldn't try to shock people. I wouldn't have steaming, humping nude bodies.'

The lack of overt sex in the film does indeed run contrary to contemporary fashion. Certainly Linda Kozlowski wears some skimpy outfits, but she never takes them off. The movie is more innocent than the average Disney film these days. Paul says he didn't set out to make quite such a wholesome and old-fashioned film, it just turned out that way. 'I think that a lot of the wholesomeness of the character is taken from Australian outback people. There probably hasn't been a hero who was this much of a gentleman since the old John Wayne movies.' Although it is classified as an 'adventure movie', Paul points out that his hero only draws his knife once. 'He doesn't find New York a hostile town because he goes in with an open mind. That's what I found. I expected to see a queue of muggers at the airport, because that's the picture everyone paints of New York. The muggers must have been on strike when I was there, because it was as open and friendly as any city. Seven million people live there. They're not all criminals.'

Above all, Paul wanted to make a movie he could show his kids, and his grandchildren. 'There are a lot of bad role models out there,' he says. 'You're putting into a kid's head that if you want to grow up to be a man you have to carry a machine gun and spend half your life in a health studio. You're telling them the more people they kill, the more of a man they are. I don't want my kids to turn out like little Arnold Schwarzeneggers.' He was taking something of a gamble, making such a film with no murders, no Libyan terrorists, no Mafia, no major confrontations. But he was proved to have guessed right.

The film opened first in Australia in April 1986 and audiences loved it. Some of the local critics, as Paul expected, panned the movie – but the rest liked it, somewhat to his surprise: 'I thought they'd hammer it. I've seen some of the Australian films that they like and they're always the ones audiences stay away from in droves. Let's face it, an Australian film should be deep, meaningful, slow. Preferably boring. Our film turned out better than they expected.' Some American critics also puzzled over the movie's obvious audience appeal, so out of sync with such trendy films as *Blue Velvet*. Paul had an answer to that: 'I haven't seen it, but *Blue Velvet* has probably been good for us. After you've come out, from what I hear, you need to have your soul cleansed. And for that, my simple little comedy's just the thing. So they went to see my film.'

Americans weren't the only people outside Australia to like *Crocodile Dundee*. In Britain the movie took off like a kangaroo. In West Germany, audiences pushed it to the top of the box-office ratings. In Italy it became the top-rated movie during its first weeks of release. The French loved it, despite the mangling of Hogan's script into brief sub-titles. The Scandinavians rushed to see it. All over Europe the movie played to full houses. The big movie bosses started to re-think their approach. Had the Rambo craze been overtaken by a nice, ambling, friendly hero? Was the clock turning back in movieland?

Looking back on the film's astonishing success, Paul summed up his reaction: 'If it had flopped completely, I'd have had to go back to square one and say "I've lost the touch, I don't know what people like any more. I must have gotten lost in the world of show business." I always have an inner ear in the middle of the front stalls, a gut instinct for what the common man or woman wants, because for the first thirty years of my life I was a boilermaker's assistant and a rigger and a truck driver. I wasn't locked up somewhere in an attic doing dramatic art or learning to tap dance.'

The film's success has had some surprising consequences. Since its release in the US in the autumn of 1986 thousands of Americans have flown out to Australia to retrace Mick Dundee's bloodstained footsteps as – tongue heavily in his cheek – he crawled his way through the swamps after his leg was supposedly savaged by a croc. But the tourists soon discovered that all those jokes about crocodiles aren't quite so funny in real life. In March 1987, one American girl, a model from Aspen, Colorado, on safari in Western Australia, dived off a yacht into the jaws of a crocodile, never to be seen alive again. On hearing the tragic news, Paul Hogan, in Los Angeles to co-host the Oscars, warned that tourists must be made more aware of the dangers of swimming in crocodile-infested waters in Australia.

Interestingly, Paul identifies strongly with his screen character Mick Dundee. 'Dundee is a real Outback type of bloke,' he says. The 'bloke' is the traditional archetype of the Australian male. He goes back to the earliest days of the original colony of New South Wales where convicts from Britain and Ireland blended with the free settlers who had come out to Australia to start new lives, for one reason or another. It was a rough, tough society not unlike the Wild West of America, where the concept of 'mateship', toughness and a healthy mistrust of authority were the order of the day. Later the bloke partly merged with the 'larrikin', a sort of street-smart city type. Paul Hogan has been described in the role of Mick Dundee as a 'larrikin', which does fit the cheeky element in Mick, but most of all he's an idealized version of the real Aussie country bloke, a strong, silent type with a streak of decency in him which would make him share his last meal with his mate (who would have to be another bloke). But this type – the Mick Dundees of the world – are probably a dying breed or at least an endangered species in contemporary Australia, which today prides itself on being a multi-racial, cosmopolitan country with the bulk of its population living in suburban houses and apartments, watching international television, going to international restaurants, driving foreign cars and doing city things. It is only really in country areas – and the Outback – where the bloke lives on.

Paul is quick to defend his creation of Mick Dundee and the inevitable fact that overseas the character will be taken to represent the average Australian – a consequence that many Australian critics have complained bitterly about. Paul insists that there is a lot of Dundee in the Australian bloke and a lot of the bloke in Dundee. Indeed, Hogan – as our story will show – has largely got where he is today by successfully interpreting, admittedly sometimes in parody, the average Australian. He also wants to destroy the image of the loutish ocker* – 'that city-bred cretin' who 'goes overseas and embarrasses everyone'. By contrast, Mick Dundee always keeps his dignity. 'Even if he is naive and uneducated he doesn't make a melon of himself. He's a lot like me. He's got some grace. There's definitely a lot of me in the character.' And he adds: 'I wanted to create someone who is slightly ambiguous in that he is this mythical outback figure who is prone to exaggerate but he also comes through when he has to. He's a true hero, not a sort of fantasy character like Rambo. I like him better than I like myself. He's got a nice philosophy and the kind of character we all envy. He's never heard of words like 'stress' and 'clock'. He doesn't have a worry in the world. I wouldn't say he's brave – he's merely a product of his environment.'

Paul Hogan is also the product of his environment, which is Australia – or more accurately a slightly old-fashioned version of Australia. When he helped present the Oscars, he displayed no sign of fame having gone to his head. He was still the same straightforward, funny Hogan that his workmates back on the Sydney Harbour Bridge remembered. But Hoges, as his mates still call him, has come a long way. Today there is no doubt that he is an international superstar. With a sequel to *Crocodile Dundee* on the way, his name will stay up in lights for years to come. From a boy from the Australian Outback to a blue-collar rigger on the Sydney Harbour Bridge to a movie sex symbol: it's a story almost as adventurous as that of Mick Dundee. He's the most unlikely superstar in film history – yet perhaps also one of the most likeable.

CHAPTER 2

Cinderella in Hobnail Boots

PAUL HOGAN was born on 8 October 1939, at
Lightning Ridge in the State of New South Wales, one of the
strangest places on the planet, let alone Australia (which
abounds in oddities). Paul used to say the Ridge was located
'at the end of the world'. It is quite literally out in the Back o'
Bourke,* about 500 miles north-west of Sydney, close to the
border with Queensland. Discovered only in 1880, it is as
mining town – the only place that produces the rare black
opal, one of jewellery's most precious stones. It was called
Lightning Ridge because (a) it lies on a slight ridge and (b) a
flock of sheep was struck by lightning there back in the last
century. When Paul was born it was very much as it is today,
or even in 1906 when the first opal rush began – a permanent
population of little more than a few hundred souls, living in
the 40 or so firmly-constructed abodes on either side of the
single main street or in the shantytown nearby consisting of
caravans, tents and a collection of old trams that somehow
found their way from Melbourne, over 1,000 miles to the
south (and presumably over the dirt roads that were, until

recently, Lightning Ridge's only link with the outside world).

The Ridge is very much like the town where the American reporter, Sue, meets Mick Dundee in the film. There's a single hotel or pub – The Digger's Rest (with three bedrooms) – a few stores, a cafe and a garage (gas or service station). Dotted throughout the adjacent landscape are the reasons for the fame of Lightning Ridge – the 100,000 or so mineshafts down which the amateur diggers search for the elusive 'colour'. That means 'paydirt' and perhaps a piece of 'potch' containing an opal worth $5 or $50,000. Paul's father, who had a transport business and ran the local mail run, would pick up the latest gossip about finds as he went about the town and its peculiar environs. One day he heard some happy personal news from the local bush nurse: he had an addition to his family, his second child, Paul.

Before we leave Lightning Ridge with the Hogan family it is worth noting that the picture Hogan paints in *Crocodile Dundee* of the Outback and its rough and ready inhabitants is deeply conditioned by Lightning Ridge and its many counterparts all over Australia. (Its Aboriginal name, by the way, is Wallangulla). Here the summer temperature goes over 120°F and it is often 75°F in winter. The local water is from artesian wells and the swimming baths, just outside the town, are sometimes too hot to swim in. One day it's a sleepy country hamlet; the next day 1,000 or 10,000 people descend on it at the hint of an opal strike or the rumour of a big find. The main sports are drinking, driving souped-up cars up the road to nearby Walgett and watching the goat races down Opal Street during the Lightning Ridge Festival in August. Until recently the town had no power and the night and the mines were lit by candles or paraffin-fuelled hurricane lamps. Flies followed you everywhere, even to the dances at Bill Waterford's Wool Shed a few miles up the track, a milieu

that Paul captured superbly in one of the opening scenes of
the movie. Yet Paul did not get much chance to enjoy the
delights of life in Lightning Ridge, for his family departed for
the western suburbs of Sydney when he was less than a year
old. The Second World War had broken out and his father
felt it was time to go back to the Big Smoke – Sydney – and
join the Australian Army.

Not a great deal is known about Paul's forebears except
that – according to one story he tells – his great-great-
grandfather was a Liverpool Irishman who was deported
from England to the penal colony of New South Wales as a
convict in chains. Paul makes light of his grandfather's
criminal record, explaining: 'It must have been a terrible
offence like forgetting to feed his dog or burping in church'.
Not much is known about Paul's own early years either. He
seems to have only ever given one or two interviews in which
he reveals anything about his childhood. One rare glimpse
was given in a series of articles by Fran Hernon, published in
the Sydney *Daily Mirror* in April 1981. It seems that Paul's
early boyhood was apparently just like any other average
Australian upbringing – happy and physical. A wiry, tow-
headed boy, he ran around in bare feet over sizzling tarmac
streets in summer, played games of cricket and footy, went
down to the local swimming baths, and during his school
holidays enjoyed days out to places like the zoo or Luna
Park, ferry trips across Sydney Harbour to Manly and perhaps longer excursions to the National Park or the Blue
Mountains and the 50 or so beaches that lie along the coast
north and south of beautiful Sydney.

The suburb Paul's family settled in after leaving Light-
ning Ridge was Granville, an unpretentious place on the
Western Line, the train track that snakes out from Sydney's
Central Station to the outer suburbs and the old city of
Parramatta, to Penrith on the Nepean River and to the cool

Blue Mountains beyond. Granville is a major rail junction, most famous for a terrible rail disaster in the mid-1970s when a road bridge collapsed on the commuter train from the Blue Mountains (the two regular commuter trains were dubbed the Fish and the Chips). It is a suburb of bungalow-style houses and quiet streets lined with gum and other trees that provide a little shade against the fierce summer heat, which in Granville is seldom relieved by the sea breezes that peter out before reaching this splendidly-named suburb. Lower middle class was probably its socio-economic classification, certainly not a slum like some of the inner Sydney suburbs such as Redfern, but not as genteel as some of its neighbours – Homebush, Strathfield, Croydon or Burwood.

It was in this environment that young Paul, now the middle child in a family of three (his brother would become a salesman of electrical goods in Canada, and his sister would marry a famous Australian Olympic swimmer, John Devitt) grew into a teenager. He got into a lot of scrapes. Looking back on his childhood, Paul recalled that he never got into any *real* trouble, 'but every time I threw something, a ball or a stick, it went through a window, or cracked open some other kid's head and then my mother would hear about it.' He describes himself, in retrospect, as a slightly eccentric child. He was rather brighter than his school-mates (though he quickly learned to disguise this shameful fact). 'I was a know-all,' he recalled later. 'They used to send me home because I argued with the teachers.'

It was a simple time in Australia, before local TV started. The high spot of the week was Saturday afternoons when all the kids would rampage round the stalls of the local Granville Civic cinema, stuffing their mouths with candy – Jaffas and Minties – and watching the Saturday children's matinee with five serials and 23 cartoons plus newsreel. At secondary school at Marist Brothers in nearby Parramatta, Paul's teachers made the discovery that he was bright. He used to score in the 90s out of 100 for English, a subject that has always been taught well in Australian Catholic schools. 'I got on all right at school,' he said. 'I just found it boring.' It turned out that he had an IQ of 140 plus – genius rating. Nevertheless, he quit school at 14. 'My parents were furious. They had great hopes for me to become a lawyer. All the vocation tests showed I had the ability. But I was sick of sitting around in stuffy classrooms. So I left.'

A couple of Paul's mates that he grew up with surfaced again later in his life. One of them was Dennis Johnson, an executive at the Brisbane broking firm of Paul Morgan and Co Pty Ltd, which, as it turned out, had a major role in Paul's later success: the firm underwrote the *Crocodile Dundee* project. The other old school-chum was John Davis Slade, whom Paul knew as Jack Slade, a name more in keeping with such an egalitarian place as Granville. 'You don't go walking around Granville called John Davis Slade,' Jack recalled later. They remained friends after Paul left school and at one stage shared a job collecting oil samples for testing at the Shell oil refinery in the nearby suburb of Clyde. Jack Slade did the night shifts and Paul Hogan did the day shifts. Jack recalled how he and Paul would sometimes put on their glad rags and go to the Spaghetti Barn in Parramatta Road. 'And I remember we were the ants' pants having a drink at the Jungle Bar of the Menzies [a poshish Sydney hotel].'

After their jobs at the oil refinery, Jack and Paul's ways parted. Jack went to Canada and later moved on to New York where, ironically, he got a job as desk clerk at the Plaza Hotel in Central Park South – the starting point of Mick Dundee's Manhattan adventures. Jack ended up working for the Marriott hotel chain and today he is a vice-president of the company, responsible for marketing in, among other places, Australia. He and Paul kept in touch over the years and recently they met again in Sydney for a slap-up meal at one of the city's more exclusive establishments – two boys from Granville who had made good. Yet despite Jack's cosmopolitan life he, like Paul, retains his Australian down-to-earth attitude: his villa in Portugal is called 'Casa Parramatta'.

Around the time when Paul and Jack's lives began taking divergent paths, Paul decided to give education another go. He started a course as an apprentice moulder, which meant going to a local Technical (vocational) College four nights a week. 'But that got as boring as school, and after a while I chucked it in.' Next he took a job at the local Granville swimming baths. His teachers and parents were not happy, and for some time afterwards Paul was held up to other boys as an example of how to go about ruining your future life. Paul recalled later: 'I was still bored at Technical school so I just chucked it in.' He had, however, found something far more to his liking in the job at the local swimming baths. This didn't please his parents either, but Paul saw it rather differently. 'There I was, wanderin' around in the sun, practising my divin', chattin' up the birds. It looked like a great life to me mates.' It was down at the Granville Baths where Paul, in between hosing down the changing rooms and practising his diving – he won a few championships – spotted a particularly attractive blonde sheila.

'I thought, "Cop that great-looking bird,"' he recalls, and he went over to chat her up. He thought she looked like a 'real little water rat', just like he was. Her name was Noelene and she was 16. They started dating. Noelene later got a job as a telephonist at Sydney's General Post Office, and two years later, when she was 18 and Paul barely 19, they got married. Paul said later: 'Our prospects were zero.' But they eventually got a Housing Commission (government-subsidized) house at Chullora, not far from Granville, and settled down to family life. Settled down, however, is probably not a good description of Paul Hogan's life at that time. He was the scourge of the local cops, doing daredevil stunts on his motorbike and generally carrying on like a typical 'Westie' (a rough type from Sydney's western suburbs). 'I used to get dressed up in all the galah* gear and roar around makin' a big fellow of meself,' he recalled. Not long before he had met Noelene he had been caught by the cops doing a handstand on the handlebars of his bike. They made him wheel the bike from Parramatta to Granville and kept on his heels all the way home. Finally the local sergeant laid it on the line: Paul had notched up $800 in fines and was about to lose his licence for 12 months, but if he gave up riding his bike, they'd call it quits. Paul figured that it was better to relinquish the bike.

When he was 20 he was called up to do his National Service training in the Army (he later joined the CMF – Citizens Military Forces – and did part-time soldiering with them for 10 years). He had given up his job at the baths after a while, finding it just as boring as his other attempts at discovering a career. He just bummed around, taking one low-skilled job after another. By the time Paul was 22 he and Noelene had three kids – all boys, named Brett, Clay and Todd. They lived in their meagre Housing Commission house made of fibrous cement and found it difficult to make ends meet. It wasn't an easy life for them, especially for Noelene, trying to bring up three young children on a labourer's wage and little prospect of them ever getting much more. In summer their fibro house was stiflingly hot. In winter with the westerly winds blowing over the Blue Mountains from the vast interior, the house was often frigid. And Chullora wasn't even as nice a place as Granville.

*   *   *

The first signs of a change in their life came late one night when Paul, lying on a bar-room floor after a punch-up, looked up to see his wife looking down at him with a contemptuous expression on her face. 'It was so embarrassing,' he said later. 'I didn't go home for two nights. But it changed me. Suddenly I realized I was meant to be a husband and a father and not a mug lout.' He began to take stock of his life and tried to reform himself. But he still had no steady job. Often he was totally unemployed. He moved from job to job, rarely staying for more than a few weeks, digging holes here or doing a few days on a building site there before moving on. Sometimes he was sacked for 'horsin' around.' 'I was a real mug lair in those days,' he recalled. 'I had a wife and three kids to support. I just didn't want to grow up.' He found labouring work boring and admits that he must have been a very difficult person to work with. He tried truck driving and, for a period, working in a shop behind the counter. He'd go out with the boys, playing his role of good ole 'Hoges', and get drunk, but it didn't really solve anything for him.

Despite pressure from his family, Paul could not see why he should compromise by trying to get some lowly white-collar clerical job and 'get soft'. Looking back on those days, he said, 'I had a lot of friends and work acquaintances that were sort of two-bob nobs. They'd look down their nose at you if they had a brand new Kingswood (car) and yours was seven years old. Or if your house was fibro and theirs was brick veneer. So they had to work a bit more overtime or work in a job they didn't like so much, just to keep five feet ahead of you. I've never been interested in being five feet ahead. I'd like to be one hundred yards ahead.

'The simple life to me means not having to work and the freedom to say no. Or get up when you wake up. That's my go. Havin' no money was a plus in one way because I could never go to the pub after work every afternoon – I used to occasionally, and get wiped out like everyone else and it was good fun – but mostly I had no money so I'd knock off work and go straight home. And the kids were always waitin' in the front yard with the football under the arm, so the minute I was in the yard I was out back with the football. Probably if I'd had a better job, as it's called, with twice as much money and some market responsibility I'd have been at meetings or entertaining clients or doing something along those lines. And I would have missed out on all that fun with the kids.'

Despite his tricky financial situation, Paul became a dedicated gambler. He managed to accumulate a betting fund of around $1,800. 'That was me punting money. It was sacred. I'd blow heaps on the horses but if anyone asked me to buy a pair of shoes I'd say I couldn't afford to pay for them.' He only finally gave up punting when he blew the lot on two consecutive Saturdays. Looking back on his gambling days, he realized that he did it mainly out of boredom. 'All the things I did then were just attempts to get out of the rut. I wanted a challenge – something exciting. Instead I used to get into a bit of bother. It was an embarrassment.'

At one stage he launched into a chequered career as a boxer. He was a light welterweight. He started fighting amateurs as a lurk* to divert the cops at an SP bookie's establishment. 'There was this SP bookie joint in Granville in a gym that had just opened up. I used to be a regular there, naturally. Me and a mate provided the cover. We'd be standin' around bettin' when the shout would come that the cops were on their way.' Paul and his mate were permanently attired in shorts, with boxing gloves at hand in case of such an emergency. As the cops arrived, the pair would hop into the ring and 'beat the livin' daylights out of each other' while the punters watched with inordinate interest 'as if we were Joe Frazier and Muhammad Ali'.

This whetted Paul's interest in the sport and he went into serious training. There is some dispute over how many fights he won. Some reports say he won 19 out of 24 fights before coming up against some tough pros and throwing in the towel. Other accounts only give him three wins. Although he wasn't a bad boxer he didn't always come out of the ring totally intact. In fact his nose got broken so many times he can, to this day, push it right into his face until it is flat.

It was around this time that he began working for the New South Wales Department of Main Roads as a plant operator. When the workers on the Harbour Bridge needed equipment, it was his job to take it to them. He also ran messages. As usual, he soon found that pretty dull. One day, however, a call came in for his boss, who was out. Paul answered the phone and heard that the caller wanted to know if anyone might be interested in a job vacancy on the bridge as a rigger (helping to maintain the bridge). 'I said I did know someone, and went over and applied for it myself.' It was the start of a 10-year career. He was 30 years old and he could look back on 40 jobs: 'For 30 years I stumbled along in a never-ending rut with nowhere to go. I was a Cinderella in hobnail boots.'

CHAPTER 3

Coathanger

THE MOST FAMOUS object in Australia – apart from Paul Hogan and the Sydney Opera House – has long been the Sydney Habour Bridge, affectionately known as 'the Coathanger'. It bestrides Sydney Harbour – known as one of the natural wonders of the world – like the Colossus of Rhodes, joining the two sides of Sydney, north and south, with a 1650-foot steel arch, still the world's largest. Originally costing £10 million, it was built between 1923 and 1931 and was opened in mid-1932. It carries eight lanes of traffic and two railway tracks, and more than 200,000 vehicles cross it every day. Such a structure, needless to say, takes a lot of maintenance. To stop it rusting it has to be painted almost continuously, all six million rivets and 52,000 tonnes of steel. Putting on the necessary 30,000 litres of grey paint each year is the job of the painters and their supporters, the riggers, the job Paul applied for, and got.

The Bridge is not only an object of affection. It's also the butt of jokes. Like a lot of Australian humour, this example relies on use of slang and idiom to put over something that might otherwise seem in bad taste (the Australian sense of humour relies heavily on irony): A girl becomes pregnant and suggests to her boyfriend that they should get married. 'No way,' says he, 'I'm not the marrying kind.' 'In that case,' she replies, 'I'm going to jump off the Harbour Bridge.' 'That's what I like about you, Shirl,' says the dinkum Aussie. 'You're not only a bonzer root but you're a good sport, too.'

Working high up on the Bridge gave Paul a new perspective on life – literally and figuratively. Instead of working down holes among the foundations of construction sites, there he was, looking across at Sydney's growing number of skyscrapers and down at the ferry boats on the harbour and the cars, taxis and pedestrians crossing the Bridge. It kind of made a bloke perk up. He would set off for work at 7:30 a.m. and knock off around 4:00 p.m. He worked rigging pulleys and planking for the painters to work on, clad in his habitual uniform of shorts, singlet (in summer anyway) and heavy boots (for protection). He was bronzed and fit and soon was scrambling over the six-inch-wide girders like a monkey. 'It was a safe enough job once you adjusted to it,' he says. 'It's no more dangerous walkin' across a six-inch girder 400 feet up than six inches off the ground.'

He might have stayed on the Bridge until he retired – it was a job for life, as the task of painting the Bridge never ended. In fact he stuck to the job for almost a decade, give or take a few excursions to pastures new. He tried other jobs on building sites, waiting cannily until the building had reached over 20 storeys so as to pick up danger money. Still restless, he tried working for his union, but found that all he was expected to do was run round as a debt collector. He returned to the Bridge, still wondering how to burst out of the straitjacket his lack of formal education had imposed on him. 'I was a pretty frustrated bloke. I don't know why.

. . . No outlet, I guess. I had a fairly short temper and did my block* over little things. I was never a big drinker but in those days I was a happy drunk when I did have a couple. Sober, I was aggressive.'

One thing he could do well, all his workmates agreed, was to be very funny, shouting out quips and jokes to his fellow riggers. Some of his mates, who are still working on the Bridge, maintain he was even funnier in those days than he was later. One of them, Derek Quinn, recalled: 'Up here on the Bridge he'd crack a smart-alec remark about somebody and they'd come back at him and he'd immediately come back with an answer. He was very quick-witted. Half the people he later made fun of on TV actually worked here. In his early shows his characters all came from here.'

One of his best mates was a bloke called Athol Gilmore, who has kept in touch with Paul since they both left the Bridge. Athol ended up running a pub in a sleepy little town in north-west New South Wales. Paul continued to invite his old mate down to Sydney for 'a beer and a good yarn,' Athol said. 'He was a joy to work with. He was funny, and he was funny all the time. He's a wonderfully gifted person. He can do anything. In a way, he was difficult to get to know because he irritated a lot of people. He'd say, "Oh, I can do that" and people would say he was big-headed, but he was just stating a fact.'

Athol says that Paul changed the work methods of the riggers too and brought them up-to-date. 'They were doing things in the same way as they did in 1930 and he'd say to me: "God almighty, Gilly, we're doing this the hard way."' Paul would then think of something else that was quicker and better. Paul was also something of a Robin Hood. He'd stand up for the underdog even if that didn't make him popular.

Paul and Athol used to take time off from working on the

Bridge for a bit of 'galah watchin'' – observing how people in different jobs and occupations went about their business. This would yield invaluable material for some of Paul's later TV skits. Indeed, one of his early characters, Good Lookin' Gilly, was based on Athol himself. It was a send-up of Athol's self-mocking vanity when he'd stand in front of the mirror in the men's room, combing his hair, something that Paul had observed at first hand. He recalled that 'Athol used to stand in front of the mirror pretendin' he was handsome – which he wasn't – and when he heard the other guys comin' he'd start to fuss with his hair and grin at himself. The others used to laugh at him, but really, he was laughing at them. We became good mates.'

Others who knew Hogan at the time agreed with Athol's analysis of him. Alan Huxton, who used to have a few schooners with Paul at the Greenacre Hotel, recalled: 'He's been painted as a loud-mouthed, macho man but that's bullshit. He was the same as everyone else. He'd have a few schooners and then go home to his family.'

Life up on the Bridge brought its dramas for Paul. The Bridge was a popular spot for suicides. People would climb from the pedestrian walkway up onto the girders, and then threaten to leap off into the water several hundred feet below. Few who actually took the plunge survived. 'We used to get people up there all the time wantin' to jump off, and I got the job of talkin' to them,' he said. Paul wouldn't mince his words: 'I'd say, "Whaddya think yer doin', yer silly bastard?" That normally stopped them in their tracks.' But on two occasions Paul's subtle approach didn't have the desired effect. On the first occasion Paul saw a bloke out on one of the four pylons at the other end of the Bridge, 'ready to go.' So Paul went into his regular routine, lighting up a cigarette – 'that was part of the act' – and strolling out onto the ledge near the would-be suicide. 'He was screamin',

"I'm goin' to jump! I'm goin' to jump!" So I said, "No you're not, yer silly bastard." Then he just stepped off into space. He fell onto the concrete. I tell yer, my 'eart practically turned over.' It made Paul realize, for one thing, how close he and all the other workers on the Bridge were to a similar fate if they missed their footing.

Even more alarming was the time when Paul risked his life to talk a man down. Paul and his mates were sitting in a crane that goes over the top of the Bridge when they spotted a young man hurrying towards them. 'We thought, here comes a jumper, because they get a certain look about them, you can tell 'em a mile off,' Paul said. So Paul got ready to go into his routine. He instructed his workmates to wait while he went up and talked to the man. He told them they must be ready to grab the man and hold him down until the police arrived. But as the man approached, he got bigger and bigger. Suddenly they realized that he was enormous – much larger and stronger than any of them, almost half as big again as Paul (who is not a particularly large man). 'He was a really massive bloke,' Paul said. 'With great big shoulders on him.' Paul asked him where he thought he was going. The man replied, 'Get out of my way!' Paul gave the boys the nod, but they didn't move. So he nodded again. Still they didn't respond. They all looked up at the sky or into their tea mugs, anywhere but at Paul and the jumper. 'They weren't going to tackle this big feller 400 feet up,' said Paul. Then the bloke pushed Paul aside and went on climbing up the Bridge.

'I thought, "You're not beatin' me,"' Paul said. 'So I went on up after him.' Paul grabbed hold of the railing with one hand and the man with the other. 'Me hand was clamped so tight on the railing I thought I'd leave me finger marks on the iron.' The man once again pleaded to Paul to let him jump, but Paul held on like a terrier and finally talked the man into coming down. But half way down he turned on Paul and lifted him up, growling, 'I could throw you over, you know.' By now somewhat scared, Paul told the man that of course he could throw him over, but what would be the point? The man seemed to see the logic in this and they continued the steep climb down. But when they reached the safety of the footway, however, the man went berserk. Paul's workmates and the police came to the rescue and struggled to hold the man down. 'I was hangin' on to one ankle and gettin' tossed around like a rag doll,' Paul said. The man was put into a straitjacket. Then he asked for a glass of water and proceeded to bite a chunk out of the glass, cutting his mouth. Blood spurted everywhere. They held him down while a policeman tried to remove the glass from his mouth. Then the man bit the policeman's finger. It turned out that he was a university student who'd been on drugs. 'Only 22 and he wanted to end it all,' observed Paul, who won an award for bravery for saving the man's life.

This incident happened in 1971, towards the end of Paul's Harbour Bridge career. Something more fulfilling than saving suicides had occurred, and new and exciting pastures beckoned. It had begun a few months earlier when a new talent show started up on Sydney television. Called *New Faces*, it was like the American *Gong Show*. Hopeful singers and dancers would get up and do their acts in front of a panel of professionals who would then criticize them unmercifully. It was often not a pleasant sight. The morning after the premiere of the show, Paul and his workmates were sitting on the Bridge criticizing the programme. Any mug, one of them declared, could do better than the contestants they'd watched the night before. Paul agreed – even he could. And they knocked the cruelty of the judges too. As the weeks went by Paul was egged on by his mates, who knew he could make people laugh, to ''ave a go.' Paul was particularly critical of the so-called judges: 'They persecuted the contestants for the entertainment of the masses,' Paul explained later. 'Every Sunday night it was the Christians fed to the lions. So we were sitting around at work on a Monday and the boys said that someone should give them a bit of their own medicine. I said "OK"'.

So he wrote off to be a contestant, sending in an application as 'A tap-dancing knife-throwing expert from Lightning Ridge'. His idea was that such an act would sound so unusual he might cut through the by then three-month waiting list. 'I thought, that'll get 'em,' said Paul, showing an early talent for marketing his showbiz abilities. Although the first half of his self-billing was fabricated, the Lightning Ridge part was technically true. In the event, the show's producers invited him on. He didn't go into heavy rehearsal, developing his 'act', nor did he worry too much about his costume. The carpentry shop at the Bridge knocked up a set of large knives for him. Then he turned up at the studio on the appointed night.

He recalled, 'I had these knives plus a garbage bin to put over my head and a great big pair of gumboots for me tap dancing. Other than those props, I had no plan except to walk on that show and get stuck into those dinner-suited judges and tell them what was wrong with them and how they could improve their act.' While the cameras rolled, Paul threatened the judges with his knives. 'Not surprisingly,' he said, 'the judges didn't find it hilarious. The producers had thought I was an idiot but I just went on and told the panel what was wrong with *their* performance and how they could improve it. I did the same thing to them that they did to the amateurs. They hated it, but the audience loved it.'

The next day Paul went back to the Bridge. His mates had

loved his performance and he was a celebrity on the Bridge for a day, but then it was back to work as usual. Then something strange happened: so popular was Paul's knife act that he was called back to appear on *New Faces* a second time. This time he went on as a shovel player, bashing two shovels together, once more garbed in his shorts and singlet. Again he was the hit of the evening, so the producers invited him back for the finals, where he put up a creditable performance as a 'thunderbox' player, an act which culminated in him dashing across stage and ramming his head through the wooden thunderbox to produce what he described as 'A-flat'. Most of the audience and the viewers at home hoped he'd win, but the judges awarded first prize to a serious young cello player. Paul came second, and remarked wryly later that the cello player probably ended up in the ranks of the Sydney Symphony Orchestra playing background music for Winfield cigarette ads – the brand Paul was later to make famous.

By now the showbiz bug had bitten him, and later he began making some appearances at the local RSL* clubs. One of his Bridge mates, Archie Wotherspoon, was the first person to go on stage with Hogan – at the Marrickville RSL at 3 p.m. on a Sunday afternoon. 'I was his stooge,' Archie recalled later. 'But as a comic now, I can't stand him. He was funnier on his job than what he was on TV.' Paul learned a lot from doing his club act, but he later said he far preferred doing television: 'In television the environment is just about perfect. You are surrounded by competent technicians, you get good sound, and you have control over the special techniques you can use. On a club stage you are at the mercy of too many elements you have no control over.'

Months went by after his *New Faces* success and Paul began to feel 'I'd be spending the rest of my life on the coathanger.' Little did he know that events outside his ken were conspiring to rescue him from the Bridge. Something was beginning to stir in Australia: a change in the way Australians felt about themselves, a new national confidence was beginning to emerge. It was, as the Australian Labor Party's election slogan put it, 'A Time for Change'. For over 20 years the conservative Liberal Party, led by the urbane, British-to-his-bootstraps Prime Minister Sir Robert Menzies, had held power. But some Australians had become aware that their countrymen often behaved as if they were the poor relations of the British. This was particularly reflected in the way they regarded their language. Until the early 1970s Australians tended to be ashamed of their accents. Some children were given elocution lessons and taught to speak 'like the Poms'. Announcers on radio and TV had either English accents or a local imitation thereof. Nobody thought a genuine Aussie accent sounded 'correct'. Paul – the boy who dropped out of school at 14 – was destined to become both disciple and beneficiary of a changed attitude, a new national pride that was to sweep Australia and eventually turn the former Harbour Bridge rigger into an international celebrity.

CHAPTER 4

Ockers

THIS NEW PRIDE in things that were distinctively Australian began to spread into the media. Television programmers, accustomed to buying most of their material from the USA and Britain, began to give the locals a go. People who looked and acted Australian were, almost overnight, at a premium. The character Hogan had portrayed on *New Faces* had been just that – a character, and obviously pretty raw. But he was genuinely and distinctively Australian, there was little question about that. The reason people liked his performances was that they rang true and familiar. The *New Faces* character undoubtedly had some of the real Hogan in it, but it was a send-up, a caricature based on what Paul had observed around him. As time went on he would clone this first, rough-and-ready character into a variety of further ones. Some people have assumed that Paul off-screen is exactly what you see on-screen. But Paul Hogan is no more Mick Dundee than he is completely any of his earlier characters, although all have a bit of him in them – Dundee and his original Hoges character certainly more than the others.

Back in 1971 what Paul did so brilliantly – and perhaps unconsciously – was to distil the essence of the Australian male character, part the traditional 'bloke', part a new and more urban personality, and project it as a new archetype, a role that was later to be labelled 'ocker'. Other Australians had tried to define and portray the Australian male archetype, the bloke, who, it was generally agreed, had certain traits: manliness, silence, bluff heartiness, a simple strength, an insatiable thirst for beer – and a certain streak of anti-authoritarianism.

In the early years of the century the poet C. J. Dennis thought he had captured this paragon in his famous collection, *The Sentimental Bloke*, in which he made him a rough diamond from the suburbs of Melbourne who had a heart of marshmallow. Dennis's bloke (with his sheila, Doreen) was recognized by many Australians as an accurate symbol of the Australian male, at least of the working-class variety.

Later, other writers did their best to update the image of the bloke, perhaps the most significant contribution being the Australian comedian and social observer Barry Humphries' character, Bazza McKenzie – a large uncouth Aussie innocent abroad who blunders through English society like a blunderbuss, uttering obscene oaths and chundering copiously as a result of imbibing too much of the amber nectar. But Bazza was too much of a parody to succeed as the new definition of the contemporary bloke. Hogan's singular contribution was to portray the better qualities of the original 'bloke' – the quiet warmth and decency which shines out of Mick Dundee.

At the beginning of his comedy career though, Paul was still working on the Harbour Bridge, largely unaware of the undercurrents around him. Yet he was just about to take his second major step in showbusiness. One of the people who had seen his performances on the *New Faces* shows was a bright young Australian journalist, Mike Willesee, who had recently started up a new, more Australian-style current affairs programme called, just to be different, *A Current Affair*. Impressed with this strange new creature who had made such a stir on *New Faces* he dispatched one of his reporters, Tony Ward, to interview Paul Hogan on the Harbour Bridge. Hogan outdid himself, inducing Ward to do pushups while he related his experiences of working as a rigger. One of Willesee's colleagues, a West Australian journalist called John Cornell, saw the interview and was more than just impressed. It was, said Cornell later, 'The most brilliant first interview anyone has done for television anywhere in the world.' Cornell straightaway realized Paul's potential. 'He was an original,' he said. On *A Current Affair* he and Willesee had been looking for a person who'd be the equivalent of a newspaper cartoonist – someone who could, with words instead of pictures, make editorial comments that would be both relevant and, hopefully, funny. They had already interviewed a number of actors for the job, but nobody seemed suitable and they had let the idea lapse. But after seeing the interview with Hogan, Willesee and Cornell had the inspired idea of inviting Paul to do the light commentaries.

Cornell recalled that at first Willesee was doubtful about actually signing up Paul. Cornell explained: 'Willesee, being meaner than Jack Benny in his early days, said, "I'm not sure that we'll go that far".' So Paul started off working on piece rates, earning the princely sum of $40 an appearance, although Paul didn't think it a meagre sum – he was amazed that anyone would think it worth paying him at all. From now on his custom was to knock off work at 4 p.m. and drive over to the studios at Channel 7 at Epping in Sydney, just in time to go to air. There was no rehearsal time. A production assistant would shove a topic under Paul's nose, such as:

'What do you think about the Queen's visit to Australia,' and Paul would simply let his thoughts flow, the idea being it would come out as the genuine, home-spun philosophy of a true Aussie, with the accent and manner to back it up.

Looking back, Paul recalled: 'What set me apart was that at a time when half the people on Australian TV were speaking this ridiculous Oxford English accent that they don't even speak in England – and the other half were copying a kind of Californian-American accent – I was talking like the blokes down at the pub. Like an Australian. Simple – but, believe it or not, everyone thought it was bloody amazing.' Suddenly the Australian accent sounded genuine and familiar while other accents from England and American sounded false and artificial. It was to be a crucial moment in Australian TV and culture generally, though few were perceptive enough at the time to recognize it.

For some time, however, Paul continued to combine his daytime job on the Bridge (fans who heard he did bridgework often thought he was a dentist) with his appearance on the Willesee show, doling out five minutes of Aussie-style bar stool philosophy at $40 a pop. No worries, as Paul would say, it was all in a bloke's day. Paul still didn't dare to leave his safe job on the Bridge for the bright but flickering lights of showbiz – not with a wife and all those hungry mouths to feed. He treated the TV thing as a bit of a laugh, expecting the TV moguls to 'wake up' to him any day.

The TV critics didn't see Paul lasting more than a year. They were wrong. At the end of his first 12 months on the box, Paul scooped the pool at the annual Logie Awards (Australia's Emmys), winning the George Wallace Logie for the best new talent, the Logie for best commercial, and another for *A Current Affair*. This kind of fame started to interfere with his ordinary life. Cars crossing the Bridge skidded to a halt when they spotted him. 'I started to cause road accidents,' Paul said. 'They'd drive across the bridge to see this idiot they'd seen on TV.' Nevertheless, he clung to the Coathanger, fearing that he would be 'just a flash in the pan.'

It was around this time that Paul branched out. One new venture was into advertising where he made a reputation for selling products – initially cigarettes – with his laconic, comic presentation. The advertising part of his career was to lead on to great things, and deserves a separate chapter (see 'Anyhow' below).

Meanwhile his appearances on *A Current Affair* were becoming more and more polished and popular. John Cornell recalled one particular example of the Hogan brilliance. He had asked Paul to do a spot on the show about taxation. Paul said he'd 'give it a think' and came up with a verbal sketch about children's clothing, on the theme of how, by swapping their clothes around, you could make two kids seem like eight. It ended with Paul advising viewers that if they wanted their tax rebates quickly they could speed things up by pinning a $10 note to their tax returns. In New South Wales 480 people actually followed Hogan's advice and in Victoria, 420 followed suit. This didn't go down at all well with the Department of Taxation.

Finally, Cornell persuaded Paul to quit the Bridge and go all-out for a TV career. 'I'd had 40 jobs before going into television, so it didn't worry me if the television thing didn't make it. I'd just do something else,' said Paul. 'I had nothing to lose. It wasn't as if I were giving up a promising law career or anything.' He saw himself simply as a bit of a yahoo having fun on tele. Cornell said later he didn't know how Paul had managed to put up with 10 years on the Bridge, but Paul had told him he hadn't minded it – he was practising to become a guru.

*　　　*　　　*

The time was coming for Paul to branch out again. After quitting his job on the Bridge he and Cornell decided to put together a longer TV programme – a Paul Hogan special, in fact. The idea was to string together some of the amusing skits he was doing on the Willesee show and flesh them out into an hour-long programme. The first special was shot in Singapore in early 1973 on the theme of 'How to Tour Abroad Without Making a Mug of Yourself.' While on location, journalist Gerri Willesee (Mike's sister) followed Paul around, finding that off-camera he was rather shy and withdrawn, preferring to stand alone, humming Elvis Presley or Roy Orbison songs to himself, smoking, or just gazing into the distance. She found, too, that he tended to freeze like a wooden doll in front of a still camera. 'I'm OK in front of a movie camera,' he explained to her, 'but in front of a still camera I feel like a posing male model.' Asked if this was subconscious antagonism towards the Press, Paul said, 'It wouldn't occur to you that I may lack confidence, or be shy in front of your camera, would it?'

The second Hogan special was shot in England where Paul called in for fish 'n chips with the Queen at Buckingham Palace (the Queen was impersonated by a look-a-like), advised Prime Minister Ted Heath on colonial affairs and depicted the well-known Australian feminist Germaine Greer (author of *The Female Eunuch*) shouting at a park full of people that she was an animal husbandry worker specialising in the collection of bull semen. Germaine, who had once been married to a builder's labourer, was a friend of Paul's and played the role of Strop's sister, Joan, in a series of skits in the show. Neither of these first two specials, however, were roaring successes.

Nevertheless, in late 1973 Hogan and Cornell formed their own company with the aim of producing their own show for Channel 7. It would be called 'The Paul Hogan

Show' and would consist of a series of comedy sketches starring Paul. Cornell became more and more impressed with Paul's abilities: 'I think he is the most intelligent man I know. He's got an incredibly retentive memory – he'd have 48 pages of dialogue including six or seven different sketches, and remember them. Never once did we have to stop and start because he'd forgotten a line.' Many of Paul's earliest characters were based on his mates from the Bridge, like Good Lookin' Gillie. Another was Luigi the Unbelievable, an amalgam of several of the blokes, and Nigel, a maniacally violent 11-year-old with a motorized skateboard whose mum thought he was an angel. John Cornell got into the act too. They were doing a skit on *The Godfather*, and Cornell was to impersonate Marlon Brando by stuffing toilet paper into his cheeks to recreate Brando's mumbling Godfather voice. The result was nothing remotely like the Godfather, but it did produce a new character for 'The Paul Hogan Show', Strop, who from that time on became a sidekick for Paul's most successful character, Hoges, a cocksure, brash blue-collar bachelor who spends most of his non-working hours down the pub with his mates.

By 1974 the Ocker type had become hugely fashionable. Hardly a TV commercial was made that didn't stress the Ocker element in Australian life. Actors who had previously cultivated refined English accents suddenly switched to the broad vowels and dropped aitches of the now-popular Aussie working-class accent. The craze reached its peak in 1974, dubbed 'The Year of the Ocker' by the Australian critic, Max Harris, who had no time for the Ocker and described the phenomenon: 'Ockerdom is male chauvinist piggery rampant.' Max Harris put Australia's Prime Minister-to-be, Bob Hawke, on his list of top Ockers, along with Paul Hogan, a film character called Alvin Purple and Bazza Mackenzie.

Although Hogan – or rather his main character, Hoges – was quite rightly taken as an arch-Ocker, the label is a little unfair. Hoges was part-Ocker, part Hogan. Paul told me, for example, in one interview, 'I can see a lot of myself at 17 or 18 in Hoges. I was loud-mouthed, knew everything, you know, gregarrilous. He sees himself as a knight on a white charger, righting wrongs, but he's never wrong and never embarrassed, because he thinks he's done the right thing. He's very Australian. That know-all stage that you go through. The know-all galah*. I wouldn't want to see Hoges myself more than once a week. He's not that kind of person – great fun to have at a party but he'd drive you nuts around the house. His weakest point is he's a know-all and what he doesn't know, he makes up.

'I quite like Hoges, he might be a bit loud-mouthed or pushy for some people, but there's no malice in him. He's a lot closer to my own character than, say, Warren Mitchell would be to Alf Garnett, or Gary Macdonald would be to Norman Gunston,' Paul said, referring to the English and Australian comedians, Mitchell and Macdonald. (He could easily have added the American actor Carroll O'Connor, who portrayed Archie Bunker.) 'He's a character from within myself that I control. I'd rather be Hoges than me. He hasn't got a worry in the world. No budgets or libel laws or income tax. I'm not tormented with worry but I don't get it that good. Sexually, he performs about a quarter of what he talks. And he never stops talking. He thinks the Royal Family is a bloody waste of money. But when the Queen arrives for a visit he'll be down at the quay cheering and ready to punch anyone who insults her.' Paul also outlined for me the differences he saw between himself and Hoges: 'I don't jump on the table down the pub and yell and shout and make a lot of noise trying to be the centre of attention. I'm very much a family man; Hoges has remained steadfastly single.'

Despite the lack of critical success that greeted his first two specials, Paul wasn't pessimistic about the future of his planned Channel 7 weekly shows. He felt he hadn't hit his straps yet, as they say in trotting circles. It wasn't until he managed to gain full control over the content of his shows that they suddenly improved. As time went on 'The Paul Hogan Show' became a national institution – although it took some time for the notoriously vicious Australian TV critics to appreciate him, the public took to him swiftly. He topped the TV ratings regularly in the sharklike competition of Australian television where, in a country of no more than 15 million or so people, each capital city had three commercial stations plus the non-commercial Australian Broadcasting Commission vying for a slice of the market.

After the first, still rather amateurish shows, based mainly on characters from the world he'd observed while working on the Bridge, Hogan's comedy repertoire expanded to include caricatures of well-known politicians like the New South Wales Premier, Neville Wran, and other fellow TV stars, including women. Paul did hilarious take-offs of Clint Eastwood (with his character Clunk Eastwood), John McEnroe, Mick Jagger and many others, along with the familiar Hogan characters, Perc the Wino, Sergeant Donger (the cop with a bionic beer belly), Nigel, stuntman Leo Wanker, Luigi the Unbelievable, and, of course, Hoges. At first most of the writing for these sketches was a co-operative effort, with Hogan, Cornell and Paul's favourite script writer Ken Shadie all sharing the effort, though the characters themselves were mainly Paul's inspiration. But gradually, as his confidence grew, Hogan began to assume a greater share of the scripting. And it was not only coincidence that as this process developed, so did the quality of the material. Of all his characters, Perc the Wino was Paul's favourite: 'As Perc I can roll in the gutter, get run over and sit on the ground and

I can't ruin the wardrobe. Not only that, people react to Perc, particularly when we film in the street.'

In 1976 Paul made his first special in America, a country he didn't take to immediately, feeling it claustrophobic to find every waitress and bartender aiming for stardom. Nevertheless, he and his team managed to get interviews with the likes of Telly Savalas, Rod Stewart, Britt Eckland and Hugh Hefner. It wasn't exactly a case of fools blundering in where angels fear to tread, but there was an element of sublime ignorance about this foray into American superstardom. As Paul was the first to admit, nobody in America had heard of him and 'they didn't know what the hell I was.' He explained how they managed to get so many top interviews: 'The secret is to get an important look on your face and rush in with the cameras. Never ask permission; that could be fatal.'

He particularly liked Hugh Hefner, who invited him and Cornell and a beautiful Hogan show regular, Delvene Delaney, to a party at his $5 million mansion, where topless Bunny girls lounged by the pool, attracting Cornell's hungry eyes. Cornell, in his role as the dense Strop, asked Hefner's advice on the correct way to kiss – mouth open or closed? Paul said later: 'Hef gave him a few tips and from that time the poor little chap was beating off the birds with a stick.' (One bird he didn't want to beat back was the delightful Delvene, who later became Mrs Cornell.)

Paul asked Hefner about his lifestyle: 'What's it like living here? Is it like working in a chocolate factory – you go off it after a while?'

'Not if you have a sweet tooth,' replied Hefner. The resulting special was called 'Paul Hogan Pays Back Glen Campbell'. This was an enigmatic reference to a special Glen had recently made with Olivia Newton-John.

One clear reason for the growing success of the Hogan shows – they were soon rating higher than any local show and only fractionally below the top imported shows – was the way Paul managed to stay close to his audience, both philosophically and physically. He got his humour straight from real life, watching the foibles of ordinary Australians he met, first on the Bridge and other work sites, then in the street or wherever he went. In addition, he caricatured the well-known stars – the Clint Eastwoods of the world. His skill was to be able to represent the person or symbol he was 'taking off' with minimal props or costume. He tried to find the essence of what he wanted to satirize and use that to make his points.

Paul once said, 'Even with make-up I don't necessarily look like the person. I just want to give a quick impression of identity. If I come on wearing a headband, a curly wig, tennis gear, carrying three rackets and scowling, everybody knows it's John McEnroe. You've created the impression and – even though you don't look much like him – you've hopefully got the audience in.' Paul further believes that one clue to his success is that he takes his comedy seriously. 'I try to avoid making it painful for anybody. It's not always appreciated, but I do take great pains to avoid hurting anyone with what I do.'

Despite the eventual success of his shows in the ratings, the Australian TV critics still carped. 'Square Eye', a puerile TV column in the Sydney *Daily Mirror*, opined in April 1974: 'Even Mr Hogan himself occasionally shows signs of having picked up some faint traces of professional polish, but his offsider, Strop, is the most unimaginably bad news. We are easy-going people in Australia and something – perhaps our rough and ready pioneering background – has given us a tolerance of untrained performers who have a shot at entertaining us. Enough is enough though, and, in my view, Paul Hogan is more than enough. Too much, in fact.'

Despite the critics, however, Paul was going from strength to strength. With John Cornell now his business partner, he had the security of sage advice and management, allowing him to get on with the creative side. Both of them were still experimenting with ways of exploiting the comic genius they had uncovered. They took a stage show called *Anyhow* (based on the catchphrase from Paul's cigarette ads) around the country. Then they took time off to make an Ocker recording of an EMI disc of *Peter and the Wolf*. Paul likened the duck in *Peter and the Wolf* to a typical Aussie 'galah'. The duck, he said, 'was behind the door when the brains were handed out.' His amiable comments about the various characters in *Peter and the Wolf*, spoken in his distinctly un-highbrow accent, endeared him to thousands of Australian schoolchildren.

That same year, 1974, English scriptwriter Johnny Speight, who wrote *Till Death Us Do Part*, described Paul as a 'pure comic genius'. Paul was by now a popular pundit and he didn't restrict his comments on the arts to just music. He gave his opinion in no uncertain terms about the American painter Jackson Pollock's work, 'Blue Poles', which was purchased under the auspices of former Australian Prime Minister, Gough Whitlam, for A$1.3 million. In his best Hoges voice, Paul, looking at the painting which is an intricate criss-crossing of dribbles of paint, exclaimed: 'It's bloody incredible. Gough must have been full, was 'e? Chalky Hill, who works on the Bridge, would have knocked up something like that for $25. The Government orta sell it while they're in front. Old Jack Pollock finished up with Blue Poles because there was more blue paint on his brush than any other colour. It looks like the mess I've seen in the paint shed down at the Bridge.'

It was all good fun, but behind the scenes a lot of people were beginning to see financial potential in Hogan. In 1974 an unpleasant little episode occurred when Channel 7 and Channel 9 competed for his favours. On 27 May Paul signed a deal with Channel 7's arch-rival Channel 9 to make 30 programmes. He was to receive $19,000 for each of the first 10 and more in the last two years. But on 4 October in the New South Wales Equity Court, Mr Justice Holland heard arguments that Hogan was bound by a verbal agreement he had made with Channel 7. Eventually Channel 9 prevailed, to the extent that the newly-appointed general manager of Channel 7, Ken Stone, felt he had to resign. The deal with Kerry Packer's Channel 9 network was sealed with a mere handshake.

Paul was starting to branch out in all directions. In 1975 he and Cornell opened their own restaurant, the Aphrodisia Rhythm Restaurant in Sydney. Paul, who a few months earlier had presented the great comedian Danny Kaye with a chiko roll (a popular antipodean delicacy, almost as popular as the famous 'floater'*), representing it as Australia's leading gastronomic delight, was suddenly presenting a menu of French provincial food at extremely low prices – the result of a lot of research done by himself and Cornell on their travels. He did feel, however, that he ought to try and play down the French side of things a little by giving out his favourite recipe: 'Prawns, the gourmet delight, can be prepared in many spectacular ways. My particular exotic favourite: Take two slices Tip Top bread. Cover with butter and stuff between the slices with the maximum number of prawns. This will vary with the size of your mouth. Remember to remove the heads as it's off-putting to have a sandwich looking back at you!' That year, he also interviewed (seriously) ex-Prime Minister John Gorton and even the critics felt he'd done a fine job, widening his repertoire.

Paul's other extra-curricular activities including doing work for charity. He and some friends started the Variety Club of Australia to help children, and he often donated his time to events in aid of charity, like the cricket match against the Poms (the English) in January 1975 when Mr Paul Hogan captained a brilliant Australian XI (actually it grew to XIV) team including Prime Minister-to-be Bob Hawke, Bazza McKenzie, in the form of actor Barry Crocker, *Rocky Horror Show* actress Kate Fitzpatrick, and John Cornell. Barry Humphries turned up at half-time, asking what he could do to help, and ended up watering the pitch. Hogan's team beat the Poms, who included top cricketer Tony Greig, and more than half a million dollars was raised in aid of the Spastic Center (a local Sydney charity) and the Darwin Appeal to help the victims of the cyclone which had recently flattened the city of Darwin up in Mick Dundee territory. On yet another occasion, Paul donated two of his most prized possessions, his two-up pennies (two-up is an Australian betting game played by throwing up two pennies and seeing which way they come down) to be auctioned in aid of the Benevolent Society. 'There can't be anything Paul treasures more,' said the Society's spokesperson, Elizabeth Masters, probably tongue-in-cheek.

But charitable activities aside, the TV work was taking up most of Paul's time. For more than 10 years he managed to keep up a gruelling pace, first with Channel 7 and later with Kerry Packer's Channel 9. By this time he was doing a large amount of the writing for the shows as well as performing. He normally said it was all a cinch, no worries. But once or twice he confessed to being on a treadmill and that the writing was the hard part, the performing was a ball. Of course he had scriptwriters to help him but the perfectionist in Paul knew that he performed his own words best. For Paul, that writing was becoming the harder part.

Yet he was proud of the writing work he did. 'I'm quite willing to cop criticism of myself as a performer,' he said. 'But I know that my writing is what I do best and at that I'm very good.' Then he added: 'I've survived because I can write. If I hadn't been able to write I would have disappeared from *A Current Affair* inside three months.' He was particularly proud of the fact that he had written – this was in the late 1970s – more than 50 hours of TV comedy since he began his career in 1971: equivalent, as he put it, to more than 25 full-length movies. 'That 50 hours mightn't be much if you're writing a soap opera. But when you've got to come up with a funny line every 20 seconds, it becomes a tremendous load. If you're just working in clubs or on stage you can use the same material over and over for years. In TV you do it once and then it's stale.'

From 1979 on, Hogan and Cornell shrewdly angled half of each show towards overseas viewers, with the aim, which was soon successful, of selling edited versions abroad (eventually more than 25 countries took versions of the 'Paul Hogan Show'). The shows became ever more adventurous in their subject matter. Australian and international televions and movies were sent up unmercifully in skits featuring 'Filth Wars' and 'Benny Five-O', and in a satire on Disney movies, Hogan found a dog with no talent whatsoever. Everyday life, too, got the Hogan treatment. 'Divorce: Australian style' had the wedding guests reassembling to get their gifts back; in a surreal skit Hogan, presented as a very small TV investigative journalist, probed the phenomenon of big eaters in a set where everything was gigantic. Sitting at a giant desk with a huge pen and huge glass of water, the diminutive reporter interviewed 'Fatso'. Not all his skits came off, but a growing number were showing signs of real genius.

Around 1979 Paul retired his Hoges character for a couple of years, feeling the Ocker syndrome had been done to death, perhaps murdered by all the other people who had jumped on that bandwagon. John Cornell's character, Strop, continued in the shows until Cornell retired from the screen in 1980 to spend more time being Paul's manager. Then actress and former model and Bunny girl Delvene Delaney acted as Hogan's foil, displaying a fine comic talent herself.

With careful calculation, Paul and Cornell tried to pace themselves so as not to burn out. They knew how fickle the public is towards showbiz heroes, and they also knew how exhausting personally it is to keep up the gags and skits week in, week out. With the agreement of Kerry Packer, who had signed their deal with just a handshake, allowing Paul to make as many or as few shows as he wanted each year, Paul started to spread out his performances. 'Some people at Channel 9 may have thought I was just lazy,' he said. 'But it was really the "retire as you go" syndrome. Me old man fell down dead when I was 20, still waiting for his world discovery tour. I decided not to wait.'

CHAPTER 5

Noelene

WHILE PAUL was climbing up the ladder of fame his family had remained very much in the background. Indeed, he had something of an obsession about his privacy. Clearly the increasing affluence of the Hogan family had meant many, mainly pleasant, changes. They had moved house several times, first from Chullora. Then, as the money rolled in – carefully husbanded by manager Cornell and a team of financial advisers – they moved up in the world to Seaforth, on the north side of the Harbour. Their tastes weren't lavish. 'We lived quietly,' said Paul. 'I don't spend much on myself. You've seen how I dress, I'm still a mess. My wife doesn't spend much on herself, but now we've got a bit of money she does occasionally spoil the children. I won't say we live cheaply. Nobody who's bringing up five kids can live cheaply. But we live pretty modestly.'

By 1978 they found their home in Seaforth too exposed to the public gaze, so they bought some land in an area further north called French's Forest and began building their own house in a place called Belrose. 'People will have a party and drive around at two o'clock in the morning and shout out things like "Good on yer, Hoges." We like to sleep at night.' Belrose was more secluded but is in a notorious bushfire area, and the new house was barely completed when it almost burned down in the fierce bushfires of 1979–80 (summer in Australia is December–February). Paul evacuated his family for 48 hours and then went back to help fight to save his house from the encroaching flames. 'There I was running around like a maniac with a garden hose putting out spot fires,' he recalled, 'there's eight other blokes trying to protect the rear of the property and I get a call from the TV station asking if I'd pose for some photographs! You can imagine it: me standing saying "'G'day viewers" and looking pretty for the camera, with the joint burning down behind me. I'm afraid I wasn't very polite on the phone.'

Inevitably, as he grew more involved in TV, Paul brought his work home with him – it was so much part of his life. Often he would test out sketches on his family. He found that if his kids laughed, the public did too. One person who didn't laugh, however, was his wife, Noelene. Partly it was because she didn't share her husband's irreverent outlook on the world. 'Our senses of humour don't coincide at all,' he was once quoted as saying. But in reality it was more serious than that. Paul Hogan, like many Australian blokes, tended to think of 'the little woman at home' as something he owned, 'like a piece of furniture', as he himself put it. This led to a slow erosion in their relationship – something that at first neither of them recognized fully. Having moved into the world of TV and showbusiness, for the first time in his life his mind was fully occupied. He had a future, and his intelligence and imagination could fly at last.

It was a classic case of one partner moving on into new and exciting pastures, leaving the other behind. Looking back, Paul is able to put the finger of blame fairly and squarely on himself. 'Comedy writers and entertainers are not great on laughs when they get home. If you are working on making people laugh all day you don't take it home with you. It's like a plumber. If you go to a plumber's house, all the taps leak. Or an electrician. His wiring's always bad and his wife's nagging him to fix it up. Comedy's the same. If your working job is making other people laugh, when you get away from it you tend to have no time left to laugh and enjoy yourself.'

Yet during those first early days of success, when the money started coming in for the first time in their lives, Paul and Noelene had still been happy together. They decided to have another baby, their fifth (their first three boys had been followed by a daughter, Lauren). Paul explained, 'The first thing we did when we started to get into some money was to say, "Let's have another kid. We can afford one now." So we had Scott, purely because we could afford him. That's one way to spend new-found wealth. I would have liked to have had six or seven kids, but that's easy for me to say. Noelene would have had to carry them.'

The early happiness with money coming in from his TV activities didn't last, however. Having found his métier, Paul's energy began to be diverted more and more into his new, exciting, glamorous career, and the humdrum of family life and a wife whom he'd been married to since he was 19 drifted into the background of his free-wheeling mind. As comedy skits and plots tumbled before his eyes, and he found himself meeting Australia's showbiz celebrities and financial moguls, Noelene was far from the forefront of his attention. He once admitted, 'I liked being a father but I knew somehow I wanted something more.'

'Looking back,' he said, 'I treated Noelene badly. There were arguments but there was never any aggro. It might have been better if there was. Instead, there was a growing disinterest from both of us, but particularly on my part.' Noelene would ask him what he wanted for dinner. Paul would be preoccupied with something and would simply answer that he didn't care. 'Or, I'd be reading and when she'd ask me something I'd mumble, "I dunno".' Although he is a man of few words, Paul can sum up poignantly the essential truth of a situation. About his collapsing marriage, he said: 'That was the tragedy of the whole thing – somewhere over those years we had lost the art of communication. Suddenly, there was hardly anything left to talk about.'

In fact, virtually the only thing they had left to talk about was divorce. As Catholics – not church-going, but still Catholics – the thought of divorce appalled them. And the family still meant an enormous amount to them. Nevertheless, they finally did get round to not merely discussing divorce, but going through with it. 'It was stupid, really,' Paul confessed later. 'Neither of us really wanted it. It was a case of an irresistible force meeting an immovable object and the divorce should never have happened.'

But divorced they were. Yet neither could get up the will to leave the family home and the kids they both loved so much. They had been married 23 years and they decided that although they had finally divorced, their love for their five kids was more important than their own welfare, so they continued to live under the same roof, but agreed to go their separate ways. Only a handful of very close friends knew the truth about their marriage that was no more. Paul, now a public figure, preferred to let the pretence that he was still happily married be the image of him in the eyes of his fans. Moreover, both he and Noelene also harboured a secret hope that maybe they might manage to patch things up.

'It wasn't as if I was out chasin' after chorus girls or anythin',' Paul said later. In fact, he and Noelene still went out together quite often, and Noelene even accompanied

Paul on an overseas trip. But it was all a sham, and it was tearing at their hearts. Paul finally decided he must try to win Noelene back. She had battled during the hard years and was the mother of their five children. She had stood by him when the going was tough. But he also knew that Noelene was a strong woman whom he had treated badly. He would have to work hard to get her back. He knew he had been a typical male chauvinist, but now, to his credit, he began to redress that wrong. For a year, he took Noelene out to restaurants, talked to her, told her about his world in showbiz and began to communicate with her again – and the old feeling of love began to return.

Finally, in April 1982, they invited 20 close friends to a party at their home. After their guests had relaxed and the food and drink was flowing, Paul suddenly got up and announced: 'Well, yers had better go into the lounge, we're gettin' married.' To most of those present this came as a total surprise – they hadn't even known that Paul and Noelene had been divorced eight months previously. A priest, smuggled into the house by Paul, conducted a simple marriage ceremony in the Hogans' living room in the presence of their five children and their guests. Then the party rolled on.

When the news trickled out and the press approached him, Paul was annoyed. He told reporters he didn't want to talk about it: 'It's like airing a domestic argument. It was sort of like, "Well, if you don't like it, why don't you get a divorce?" "Well, OK, I will." So we did. It was as silly as that. Although in her case it was more like a cry for attention, I guess, because I was totally involved in my own little world, drifting away from the family. So it was a funny divorce, a divorce where we never left home.' He believes the trouble they went through was good for him: 'It just took me that jolt to wake me up to what my life was about.'

*   *   *

Marriage, second time around, has made both Paul and Noelene 'very happy'. Paul says it was something they just had to do – put the past behind them and start again. He now tries to spend at least two months of each year 'just doing nothing, and doing it with my best girl, Noelene. Noelene is one of the nicest people I know and that makes her easy to live with, and generous to a fault, but she's normal – she doesn't want to be the centre of attention.' If anything, Paul has been even more protective of his family privacy since then. He enjoys nothing more than 'muckin' about' at his comfortable, six-bedroomed home at Belrose, with its swimming pool and tennis court – comfortable, but by no means a Hollywood-style mansion. It's a place where his grown-up kids and their families and friends can come and relax while Paul gets out his lawnmower and cuts the grass or indulges in a swim or a game of tennis. So far, his eldest son, Brett, is the only one to follow in his dad's showbusiness footsteps. Brett is a lighting cameraman and has been working with Paul on writing the script for the sequel to *Crocodile Dundee*. Clay has been working as a cab driver. Todd was a garbage collector for a while before going to England to play professional football. Paul told Bob Cameron of *New Idea* magazine in Australia that he was angry when one of Todd's mates snubbed him because he was a garbo*. One reason Todd was doing that job, explained Paul, was that he found it an ideal job for football training. 'He's a bit like me in that respect,' Paul said. 'I had 40 jobs before hitting my mid-life crisis and going into television. I was 29 then and started talking to myself in the mirror, saying all the usual things like "What's this? What am I doing? Where am I going?" The answer was nowhere.'

Not long after they re-married, Paul and Noelene became grandparents for the first time. Having married first time around so young, they found themselves, in their mid-

Paul Hogan

© World Press Network

◯n the air.

© Impact Photos/World Press Network

. . . and in the air.

Enjoying a Foster's Lager in England

© Fairfax Magazines

Paul Hogan and his wife Noelene

© Fairfax Magazines

It's a tough life! Surrounded
by beauties while perusing
"Playboy Magazine."

Paul Hogan, *right,* as an Indian fakir in a TV skit

Sir Frances Hoges, *left,* in "Paul Hogan's England"

As John McEnroe, *right,* in a skit from "The Paul Hogan Show"

© Fairfax Magazines

Paul Hogan as Hoges

Paul Hogan with friend and manager, John Cornell

Paul Hogan opening the 1987 Oscar ceremonies in Hollywood

forties, gazing with pride at their first grandchild, a girl. Paul has taken happily to being a grandfather. 'I can have a baby in the house and play with it, and when I'm sick of it I can hand it back,' he said. He doesn't mind his fans knowing he's a grandfather because he doesn't really regard himself primarily as a sex symbol, even if they do. He thinks of himself as a comedian first and foremost. 'Being a comedian is better than being a sex symbol because sex symbols get old and ragged and comedians don't. Look at George Burns . . . he's over 90, and look at Bob Hope . . . 80-plus. They still make people laugh. That's more important than anything else.'

Anyhow

IRONICALLY, although Paul's TV shows through the 1970s and early 1980s eventually led him to superstardom, it was in fact his TV commercials – both in Australia and overseas – that really gave his career the crucial boost. As soon as he began appearing on the Willesee programme *A Current Affair* it became clear to a number of advertising people that here was someone who might be able to persuade people to buy things. Yet, despite his sales appeal, Paul always insisted on choosing carefully the products he was prepared to represent. Typically, cigarettes and beer were OK with him, they were things he liked. But champagne or soap powder . . . no way, mate – he just wouldn't feel comfortable advertising them. Thus it was no surprise that the first product he chose to advertise was a new brand of cigarettes manufactured by Rothmans, called Winfield. After all, he was as keen a smoker as the next bloke. This new brand was being introduced in 1972 as a totally Australian product, no doubt because Rothmans, like many other astute companies, had sensed that suddenly Australians couldn't care less what people overseas were smoking or drinking; they now wanted all-Australian products.

Paul was doing his regular spots on *A Current Affair* and still working on the Bridge when Rothmans and their advertising agency, Hertz Walpole Campbell Ewald, came up with a slogan for the new brand: 'Anywhere, anytime, anyhow . . . have a Winfield.' Jim Walpole, a partner in the ad agency, felt that the slogan didn't sound quite right – too slick and international for a genuine Aussie smoke. Allan Johnstone, later to be a partner in the MoJo agency – more of which anon – was also working on the Rothmans account and agreed with Walpole that the ad needed a more down-to-earth touch. Walpole told Johnstone he'd seen that 'funny guy' on *A Current Affair* and felt they should try him out. They discovered that Willesee and Cornell were then managing Hogan and approached him with the scripts for the ad, which he agreed to 'have a go' at.

They dressed Paul in a dinner suit and put him in front of the Sydney Symphony Orchestra. The ad would contain an element of the send-up, a parody of all those slick cigarette ads. Walpole had feared that Rothmans would balk at using a virtually unknown rigger from the Bridge to launch their new product. So the agency first had to sell the idea to Rothmans. They made a five-minute film of Hogan sitting sprawled in a comfortable chair in an office, his hobnailed boots up on the desk. Looking straight at the camera, Paul told the executives at Rothmans exactly why they should hire him for the commercial. The managing director of Rothmans, Reg Watson, enquired who this Hogan was. Walpole explained, fearing that Watson had missed Paul's charm. To Walpole's relief, Watson replied: 'He's a very good salesman, entirely credible and spanking new.'

The resulting ad, using the shorter and more Australian slogan 'Anyhow, have a Winfield', was the start of one of the most successful advertising campaigns in Australian history. Despite advertising and movie guru Phillip Adams' lack of confidence in the ads (which he described as 'a tricky piece of positioning'), they worked. Winfield, which Paul himself always smoked – 28 a day courtesy of Rothmans – became the biggest-selling brand in Australia. And Hogan became a household name across the country.

The Winfield commercials were the first real indication that Hogan had something special – the almost unique power to put across a 'message'. The ads were variations on a constant theme: the underdog who makes it. In an early one, Paul is seen wandering into the Sydney Opera House. He starts conducting the Sydney Symphony Orchestra (which actually did play the theme music for the commercials): 'No sweat, any mug can conduct a symphony orchestra, anyhow, have a Winfield . . .' It was in this ad that he uttered one of his most famous lines. Turning to the orchestra he says 'Let 'er rip, Boris.'

One of the most elaborate Winfield commercials involved Hogan flying through the air with the greatest of ease on a circus trapeze. Producing this epic required a production team of 35, working for a full week, not to mention the combined expertise of 140 circus stars, four elephants, two camels and four horses which took part in the grand parade finale. Altogether the commercial cost around a quarter of a million dollars to produce. With so much money on the line, Paul's life was insured for around $100,000, and more than 5,000 feet of film was shot, later to be edited down to a tight 60 seconds.

It was shot in front of a live audience in the Big Top jointly used by Ashtons Circus and the Switzerland Circus Royale. The two companies suspended their own show for the duration of the commercial shoot and provided a team of experienced trapeze artists to help Hogan master the technique. Frank Gasser, a trapeze artist from Switzerland and sixth generation circus man who worked in the act on camera, plus circus manager Merv Ashton's wife Nikki, and David Fink, had to work out a method of giving Paul the basics so that he could look as if it was the easiest thing in the world, flying 25 feet high through the air, hanging from the trapeze bar. By the end of a week of practice during which Paul ripped all the muscles in his arm and had to apply ice packs every four hours for days, Ashton was surprised to find that Paul had picked up the basics of trapeze work. 'He learns fantastically fast,' he said.

Ignoring the pain of the ripped muscles, Paul had to repeat and repeat the performance until it was perfect. He remained patient, good-tempered and co-operative throughout the entire shoot. The final commercial shows him executing his trapeze act and pausing to say: 'G'day. Ya probably think I'd do almost anything for a Winfield. . . . Well, you're almost right. But what's 'appened 'ere is that Winfield's given me a chance to do something I've wanted to do for years: and that's 'ave a lash at the flying trapeze. . . . Anyhow, have a Winfield.' That particular commercial was shot in 1974 and Paul continued to make Winfield commercials, building up the brand-name's image and sales until it became the leading cigarette in Australia. His face grinned down from enormous street hoardings, from the sides of buildings, and from the big screen in cinemas. John Cornell recalled noting how great Hogan looked on the big screen, but they were too busy churning out television programmes to think seriously about making a movie.

In 1980 Rothmans and Paul were pulled up dead in their tracks by an anti-smoking lobby, the Movement Opposed to the Promotion of Unhealthy Products (MOP UP), which claimed that Rothmans should be banned from using a popular figure like Paul Hogan to advertise cigarettes because children regarded him as a hero. Part of the evidence which MOP UP presented was a survey it had made of 500 schoolchildren aged 12 to 14 who were questioned about their attitudes to smoking. The survey showed that Hogan was very popular with the children, with 71 per cent regarding him as 'terrific' or 'good'. A spokesman for MOP UP said: 'The survey showed that 88 per cent of schoolchildren knew that Hogan promotes Winfield and when the same children were asked which brand they smoked or would smoke if they were smokers, they said Hogan's.' Public feeling ran high on the subject. A leading anti-smoking spokesman, H. R. Elphick, cited M.A.S.H. star Alan Alda's comments when he turned down a lucrative cigarette commercial: 'I am not going to ask somebody to get lung cancer so I can make $50,000.'

The Australian Advertising Standards Council studied all the evidence and ruled that Rothmans were violating a clause in the Australian advertising code which stated that no advertising for cigarettes may include people who have appeal to children. Rothmans appealed for time to reorganize their advertising campaign, but for nearly four years Paul's face was no longer seen 'aving a Winfield. The advertising industry was up in arms at the ban, but Paul himself remained silent, except for the remark – justified in the circumstances – that he was the only personality ever banned from TV advertising for being too successful.

Paul and his business partner John were approached by almost everybody wanting to sell a product in Australia, but they knocked them all back, believing that Paul's image wouldn't benefit, despite the estimated millions or more they might have gleaned from the ads. It wasn't until Carlton and United Breweries approached him to help launch their Aussie Foster's lager in Britain that they began to reconsider their position. The lager, described as Australia's 'amber nectar', was to be brewed in England. Up till then it was a lager loved mainly by people in the Australian state of Victoria. Drinkers in the neighbouring state of New South Wales affected to disdain it, preferring their local beers.

In Britain, however, a promising situation existed. Sufficient Australians were visiting or living there (around 40,000 Australians alone live in London at any one time) and a lot of them thirsted after a decent, cold beer. State jealousies paled into insignificance when the Aussie traveller was forced to drink English beer – compared to that fate, any Aussie beer was infinitely preferable. Additionally, the Australian comic strip character, Bazza Mackenzie, created for the satirical magazine *Private Eye* by Barry Humphries and Nicholas Garland, consumed copious amounts of Foster's, coming as Barry did from the home of Foster's, Melbourne. This created a good base for popularizing Foster's. Secondly, a lot of Brits had begun to realize that they didn't have to go on forever drinking warm, weak local beer. Lager beer generally was rising in popularity.

Foster's decided to exploit these opportunities and did a deal with the UK brewers Watney Mann and Truman Brewers to start making their lager under licence in England. It wasn't exactly the same 'amber nectar' that the Aussies knew and drank. It had less gas in it, and tasted more bitter – to suit local tastes – but at least it was made from yeast and hops imported from Australia. Hopefully, the gamble wold pay off, despite the intense competition of 17 other local UK brewers. But it was the added ingredient of Paul Hogan that ultimately did the trick.

The Poms didn't quite know what had hit them when (despite previous exposure to other Australians, including the terrible Bazza Mackenzie) Hoges – and in this case it was a variation of the original Hoges, not Paul Hogan – started taking the mickey out of them. His approach was to take the wry, almost sardonic Aussie sense of humour and apply it to British institutions – like their notoriously damp weather, their country pursuits and their entrenched class system. Asked how the British took to being sent up, Paul said that it depended a lot on how you did it: 'Nobody wants a visitor in their house saying "This place is a dump, what awful furniture." But if they had an awful painting hanging up, you'd say, "That's pretty nice," and send it up in a mild way. The Poms invented laughter and satire.'

When around this time – in the early 1980s – I interviewed Paul in London at his swish suite at the Hyde Park Hotel, I was surprised at his attitude to the English. Paul, then 41 years old, displayed that urbanity which he has polished even more since then, without losing any of his natural charm. His wife Noelene was with him, and they'd just done a whirlwind trip round London Bridge, Westminster Abbey, the Tower of London and the Houses of Parliament. He reminisced about his first visits to England back in 1973 when he made his first Paul Hogan special.

'That first visit, for about five weeks in June and July, was pure magic,' he told me, stretching out his legs and putting his bush boots up on a chair. 'The sun shone until 10 p.m. Naturally, that was a bit of a freak, a long hot summer.' Then, unable as a Sydneysider not to take a swipe at rival Melbourne, he added: 'Normally London has more of a Melbourne climate. Wet.' He said he was delighted with the friendly response he got from the ordinary people in the street when they spotted 'that geezer from the Foster's ad' but he felt that the impact he'd had on British TV would backfire if all the rest of the Aussie Ocker brigade were to jump on this bandwagon, as they had earlier in Australia. Back home, he said, the Ocker thing had got out of control.

'There was a stage when every time you turned on your set all you'd hear was g'day, g'day, g'day, g'day – it nearly made you throw up in the end.' Fortunately, he said, this swamping of Ockerism didn't backlash on him because 'I was the only real one. The others were manufactured.'

Paul told me he liked the British-style pub. 'I mean, at home we build pubs along the principle of as much tiles and stainless steel as possible so you can hose it out at the end of the day – you know, all the blood and the spillage. That was the kind of pub I used to drink at in the western suburbs of Sydney. But here the pubs are like your own little club, your own little regular club near your office or in your own street, with a fireplace, and character and charm. And some of them are so small you have to duck under all the doorways because people were only about five foot tall when they were built.' He wasn't, of course, being entirely serious.

The pubs weren't the only thing to impress him. In telling me about his forays into English 'stately homes', he let down his guard a trifle. Hoges had been mixing with the swells. 'I've been invited to one or two stately homes. I've made a few friends. When I say stately homes I don't mean the ones that are open to the public, when I say stately homes I mean the ones the like of which we don't have at home. One of them belongs to a QC. Two of them belong to people in television, I won't name any names, they're friends. It'd be a bit crass of me to drop names. I've never done that at home. I've never been the type to ring up *TV Week* and say "I've just had Bobby Limb (an Australian TV personality) and Kamal (an antipodean singer) around to a party at my place."'

He continued, 'I've never been a Pom basher, not like Bazza Mackenzie. Hoges has never been into Pom bashing or anything. If he's bashed anyone, it's been Australians. Some people say I'm sending up Italians, with Luigi the Unbelievable, and they complain to Al Grassby (an Australian ethnic representative who supported the newcomers, such as the Italians, to Australia) but 90 per cent of the time I'm sending up ordinary Australians, and they don't mind. And if I don't do Luigi the Unbelievable any more I get Italians saying "Hey, what 'appened to Luigi?" I get a lot of Greeks, there are 70,000 Greeks in Melbourne, it's the second largest Greek city in the world, and I get taxi drivers calling out: "Hey, what about the Greeks? They'd rather you insulted them than ignored them."' Talking about the edited version of the *Paul Hogan Show* that he'd sold to Channel 4 in Britain, he explained that British audiences, being closer to Australians because of their heritage and mutual ancestry, might have been able to absorb a little more of the homegrown humour. He added, without sounding in the slightest boastful, that the show was now seen in Japan, Italy, Zimbabwe, Portugal, Spain, and Beirut. 'A lotta places they just stick it on without subtitles, but the Japanese dub it.' In Thailand, as English is the people's second language, there was no need to dub it. Paul wondered at first how they would like the show: 'I mean, you don't see many Thais having a singalong in the family car or laughing away to themselves at the traffic lights.' As it turned out, he had no worries. The Thais loved the show. 'They're half-hour shows cut from one-hour specials over the past three years,' he said. 'So in some of them I have less wrinkles.'

He added that now he was in his 40s, he had started to worry about putting on weight and had started taking up exercise. 'I'm startin' to soften up a bit as I get older,' he said. 'I was always one of those people who never did any exercise and ate anything they liked and always weighed the same from about age 18 – which annoyed the hell out of my wife!' I asked him if he saw any danger in his becoming 'Pommified' if he spent too much time in Pommieland. 'There's more chance of a kangaroo becoming Pommiefied than me,' he replied. And then he started talking about the kind of Australian who became an expatriate, 'the ones who come here and acquire an accent they think is Oxford but it's nothing, and to people here it sounds like Australians talkin' funny – they're almost as bad as the Bazzas who come 'ere and walk about in T-shirts and chips on the shoulder sort of saying "I'm an Aussie and you can like it or lump it." Certainly a lot of ignorant English people do treat you like you're bit of backwoodsy. They offer you paltry sums of money to do things you'd be insulted by at home.'

He remarked on how Kerry Packer, with his World Series Cricket, Rupert Murdoch, with his international publishing and media empire, and other Australians were making their mark, if not necessarily making friends. 'They're letting it be known we're not a lot of dummies walking around with hats with corks dangling around their brims. I like the idea of a lot of people at home squirming at the prospect of me bein' shown around the world as a typical Australian – which I'm not. But ask those same people, do you prefer Rolf Harris (Australian expatriate comedian) with his wobbleboard, or Dame Edna in a dress? They may be very funny but that's the total sample of Australian humour.' Then he added, 'Humour is an IQ test of a country. If you can laugh, nationally, at your own shortcomings, you score high.'

Paul made his views clear on a number of other aspects of British life. Girls, for example. 'Half the women in London seem to wear teatowels over their heads. I'm more used to the tanned, long-legged girls back home, they look like California girls. A lot of English girls have big busts, which I don't find attractive – so many small girls with large busts, maybe it's something to do with having to work harder to breathe here. I dunno. Legs? they're covered up more here. Because of our sun you get a chance to see more of our girls and make a judgement on 'em. Of course, like anywhere, you'll see some stunners here that make you turn around.'

The Royal Family was something he throughly approved of: 'I'm certainly not anti the Royal Family. In fact I'd say I'm pro. It's just the same as I'm pro the Tower of London and London Bridge and anything else that's around that they don't make them like that back 'ome. And they don't make people like Charlie (see "Chilla" in glossary) any more. If I lived 'ere I'd be really pro 'em as I think they're a great tourist attraction. My favourite? Oh, like everyone else, probably Di – she looks like an Aussie girl. I like Charles too, he seems like a good sort.'

One thing British that Paul could not praise, however, was the beer. 'It's flat and it's got sediment and I just don't like the taste. I've tried a lot of the traditional local beers here – they're a very acquired taste. Some of their beers look to me like somebody's ashed a cigarette in them, there's so much sediment.' On certain occasions in Britain he has demonstrated a slight case of the chip he always said he was trying to eradicate from Australians' shoulders: 'When I've been in Britain I've found that a couple of people tended to treat me as though I was not mentally very bright because I was an Australian. I'd sit here thinking, "I can buy and sell you in every facet of life but, because I don't talk like you talk, to you I sound like a dumbo." They'd have this slightly superior air but I'd soon put a stop to that by saying, "Listen, fella, I'm richer than you, I'm smarter than you, I'm better looking than you. Socially, economically and physically I'm superior to you. Aussies aren't ashamed of their accents anymore. Our rock bands have developed their own kind of music instead of simply copying England and America and it is OK to be an Australian.'

The Foster's ads – which had people turning on their TV sets just to catch them – were clever. One of them had Hoges turning up at a traditional English foxhunt, telling viewers how there's nothing like a can of Foster's after a hard day's Aussie dingo (wild Outback dog) hunt. Then he looks down at the pack of baying English foxhounds and says, 'Don't think they'll have much trouble catching that funny looking pack of dingoes.' Another ad showed Hoges standing outside a traditional English pub on a typical English rainy day, explaining how in Australia they celebrate the ending of a drought with a can or two of the amber nectar. 'You, too, can enjoy Foster's . . . now the drought has broken.'

In yet another commercial he gave a mini-lecture on the characteristics of Foster's, pointing out 'the golden amber fluid' and continuing, 'Oh, and there's this part here, the white part. It's called a head. It tastes like an angel cryin' on yer tongue, viewers.' He always acted with elaborate chivalry towards women in his commercials. In one he says, 'In Australia we look after our sheilas,' and passes a Foster's to a girl sitting beside him. The beer is decorated with a little paper parasol and some floating cherries. And a later one shows Hoges all togged out in black tie watching *Swan Lake* in a box at the Royal Ballet, accompanied by a sophisticated lady in evening dress. The ballet begins and then the male lead enters. Suddenly, an embarrassed Hoges, holding a can of Foster's in one hand, places his other hand protectively over his companion's eyes. 'Strewth,' he exclaims. 'He's got no strides on!' The British loved it.

Advertising experts agreed that Paul was the ideal person to advertise Foster's. He was masculine, good looking and funny. 'I have to admit it, we're aiming at males,' a Foster's UK advertising agency spokesman said. 'Foster's is not a ladies' drink. It's too strong.' The result, after one year of the Hoges treatment, was that 29 million pints of Foster's were being consumed annually in the London area – a creditable six per cent of the market. Paul won two British awards for his

Foster's commercials – best beverage commercial and second best commercial in any category made in 1982.

Foster's decided to go national in Britain several months ahead of schedule, and on the strength of this Paul sold an edited version of his television show to British TV – possibly becoming the first TV star in the world whose appearances in TV commercials preceded his acting debut. Paul sat back on a floating restaurant barge on the Thames, knocking back the caviar and canapes, at the end of that first successful year, and surveyed his achievement. No, he wasn't surprised, he drawled laconically. 'I know it sounds conceited, but those ads were well done.'

CHAPTER 7

Slip another Shrimp on the Barbie

Until Paul Hogan ambled onto their TV screens at the start of 1984, the average American barely knew where Australia was, or precisely which language Australians spoke, let alone who this strange creature from Down Under was. They had heard about Australia lifting the America's Cup from the New York Yacht Club the previous year. A few Americans had visited Australia on leave during the Second World War or the Vietnam War. Others perhaps had seen an Australian movie or two, or even had heard the Little River Band or knew that Olivia Newton-John of *Grease* fame had been brought up there.

Despite the fond belief held by Australians that their country was well-known and admired by the Yanks, the truth is that it had hardly impinged upon the general American consciousness, even though *Women's Wear Daily* had listed Australia as 'the most "in" place in the world' in January 1984. Yet as long ago as 1981 edited highlights of *The Paul Hogan Show* were being screened on late-night TV in Los Angeles. A small, elite group of aficionados, which included Olivia Newton-John, Paul McCartney and Elton John, began raving about Hogan, to the bemusement of their friends who didn't know him from a jar of Vegemite. Then videos of his shows were shown in the trendy LA restaurant, Spago's. But it remained the cult of a tiny minority. This inexcusable ignorance, however, was about to end.

For some while Paul had been trying to persuade the Australian Tourist Commission and the Federal Government to do something about Australia's feeble image overseas. On a brief vacation in the States he'd been miffed when Americans had asked him if he was from England. When he said he was from Australia they praised him, 'Well, gee, you speak good English.' Back at his hotel he switched on the TV set and saw an ad for Qantas, Australia's national airline. 'It had talking koalas,' he marvelled. 'I thought, what an image. I'm not flying an airline piloted by a koala!' Paul was convinced he could sell Australia: 'I thought, a blind man on a galloping horse should be able to see the tourist potential of this place. If we can't sell Australia, we can't sell anything.'

To the Australian tourist bigwigs, Paul pointed out that a country like Hungary could attract 15 million tourists a year while Australia, with its beaches and bushland and wide open spaces, was attracting no more than a million, and of that number only 130,000-odd were Americans. 'If we haven't got more to offer tourists than Hungary, I'll go heave,' he commented in his inimitable silver-tongued way. And he added proudly, 'I've been around the world a fair bit and all the beautiful sights of the world, they all look a bit average when you see what we've got in Australia.'

The interesting thing here is that, for once, Hogan was being dead serious. He told the government: 'Listen, you blokes, give Brownie (the Minister for Tourism) the money.

We can sell Australia, he and I. You can't sit round the woolsheds forever waiting for cardigans to come back into fashion.' (This was a reference to Australia's former big money-earner, wool). Hogan said it was time they realized that tourism was one of the few industries that would bring money into Australia. The Lucky Country* was down on its luck after the boom times of the Seventies. But he wasn't knocking everyone. He stood up strongly for Tourist Minister Brown for what he'd said about Australia's previous tourist ambassador, the ubiquitous koala bear. Brown had described the 'cuddly koalas' as being, in fact, 'flea-ridden, piddling, stinking, scratching, rotten little things'. Said Paul, 'He wasn't bagging koalas. The point he was making is that people won't fly halfway round the world to visit a zoo. There's a helluva lot more to this joint than kangaroos and koalas, but that's all they've seen in the past.'

With these sentiments, and the help of the local MoJo agency – whose Allan Johnston had helped so successfully with Paul's Winfield ads– Paul put together a proposal for a new kind of US advertising campaign to attract more American tourists to Australia. 'We're all personal friends and we're all sort of patriots,' Hogan explained. 'We offered our services because we know we can do it real good. I want to sell something other than beer and cigarettes, and Australia's the best product I can think of.'

Tourism Minister Brown agreed. He liked the Hogan/ MoJo approach. He shared Paul's low opinion of previous efforts to promote Australia's image in America, and he was especially dismissive of the image put out by the Australian film industry – a point that Paul Hogan was to take up later. Brown, speaking of such Australian films as *My Brilliant Career* and *Breaker Morant*, said: 'Americans expect to come to Australia and find us dressed in period costume'. Some of his cabinet colleagues, before they saw the proposed Hogan/

MoJo promotion, expected to see the old Hoges – the Ugly Ocker, nose smeared with zinc cream, dribbling beer and wearing torn shorts and army boots. What they saw instead was an altogether smoother Paul, neatly dressed in a sports shirt and trousers, quietly-spoken, sporting a friendly grin and telling Americans they were welcome in Australia where they'd find the people were friendly, spoke the same language and dressed and entertained informally in the outdoors. Paul's proposed series of advertisements was approved and he was asked to complete a test campaign to be launched in California.

It isn't widely known that Paul did not receive a single cent for making and appearing in the commercials. He explained why: 'They wouldn't have been able to afford my fee anyway.' On the other hand, his generosity was backed by a canny streak of business acumen. He said, 'I'm not going to work for a small fee and thereby reduce the price I'd charge everyone else around the world who wants me to sell something. Doing them for nothing is the best way out of it.' But he was also proud of doing something for his country for nothing. He said he would rather see the promotion's budget spent on the actual campaign, not on a huge fee for him.

And once again he had demonstrated a quintessentially Aussie and Hogan characteristic – that odd combination of generosity on the one hand and shrewdness on the other, plus perhaps a third ingredient: the diffidence Australians experience if they appear in public doing something altruistic (or unmanly). So Paul made light of his gesture, which probably cost him several hundred thousand dollars: 'I don't want to be in a loser. I've only ever sold three products in my life – Winfield, the Hogan shows, and Foster's lager, and they've all broken records. I'm not going to blow my track record and lower my price by selling something that won't work.' Tourism Minister Brown, however, had another explanation. He said that Paul, with five children of his own, was concerned about the problem of rising youth unemployment. An increase in tourism would help create new jobs. Paul's gesture was 'a very rare and generous one', said the Minister, who added that Paul was a 'skilled and brilliant communicator.' Nevertheless, many would-be cultured Australians shivered in their shoes at the thought of Hoges representing their fair land overseas. Paul was highly indignant that anyone would think he'd let the side down: 'Anybody who cringes at the thought needs psychiatric help,' he said.

In the first ad in which Paul welcomed Americans – the Yanks – to Australia, he looked directly into the camera and said, 'America, you look like you need a holiday – a fair dinkum holiday, in the land of Wonder . . . in the land Down Under.' In 60 seconds the camera panned from Paul at Ayers Rock in the centre of the Outback to the crystal clear waters of Lizard Island in northern Queensland; from a trendy pub to the famous fish restaurant, Doyles, on the beachfront at Watson's Bay, Sydney, ending with him standing on the shores of Sydney Harbour with the Bridge and the Opera House in the background offering to 'slip an extra shrimp on the barbie for ya' and inviting Americans to 'Come on down and say g'day.' (Of course, no dinki-di,* red-blooded Aussie would dream of throwing a *shrimp* on a barbie: a juicy T-bone, perhaps, but seldom a shrimp – which an Australian would call a prawn, anyway.) Coupled with a toll-free phone number for interested viewers to call, the ad was an instant success. Paul, having explained to viewers the geographical position of Australia, went on to say, 'Now if you still don't know where Australia is, it's a pretty sure bet you don't know where your phone is.'

*   *   *

Up to a thousand calls were received each time the ad went to air. Between 9 January and 22 February 1984, more than 30,000 calls were recorded. Applications for holiday visas soared by 80 per cent and airlines began to be booked out on the Los Angeles–Sydney–Melbourne run. The Americans were beginning to get hooked on the idea of the new, Aussie, frontier. MoJo's Alan Morris, pleased with the success of the commercial, said: 'So many Americans who are only dimly aware of Australia know us only as a place full of weird furry animals. Americans are now seeing a sundrenched Australia; they're seeing clean beaches, clear water, fantastic landforms, sophisticated cities and friendly people who speak their language. When they come to Australia, Americans know they are not necessarily going to find people throwing fire bombs at their embassy or burning their flags. They are going to be among people who actually like them. They're not going to be caught in a cultural trap.'(Before they made the ad MoJo consulted a communications psychologist who told them that Americans tended to be paranoic about being hated or trapped in a foreign culture.)

Paul's Aussie accent, to everyone's relief, had gone down amazingly well with the Yanks. (In one later ad he said, 'You'll have the time of yer life in Australia 'cause we all talk the same language, though you lot do have a funny accent.') An elated director for the North American region with Australia's National Tourist office, Alan Drew, said: 'America is in love with Australia and loves the accent and the phrases. There have been no problems with the accent at all. The way it is in Los Angeles, Americans can't get enough of Down Under slang and our way of talking.' And though Paul had at first thought his appeal would be greater on the West Coast because he thought the Americans likened him to a California boy, his appeal never waned when the commercials were later shown in other parts of the States.

Sparra and Brownie (Paul's nicknames for Prime Minister Hawke and Minister Brown) were tickled pink with the results. Australia leapt from No 49 to No 1 on the list of most popular tourist destinations outside of America. Qantas, Australia's airline, reported a staggering 6500 seats sold between 1 April and 1 July on its new US West Coast–Cairns (Queensland) run which began on 1 April. Even the Pacific island of Fiji – two thirds of the way across the Pacific – was celebrating. As a result of the Hogan ads, Fiji was enjoying a substantial increase in the number of US and Canadian tourists stopping over. Paul's wind was blowing everyone some good.

Not everybody, however, was singing Paul's praises. One sour note came from John Carroll, a columnist on the *San Francisco Chronicle* who echoed the irritation of many Americans: 'Let us admit it – are we not just a bit sick of the Australian invasion of our media? It seems we cannot turn on our radios or televisions these days without having some hearty male calling us "mate" and wishing us "g'day" and/or touting some product which has made millions of Australians happier than prawns on a barbie. Why us? Why now?'

Yet despite such wet blankets, Paul's popularity continued to rise. His second commercial, first shown in September 1984, showed him spit-polishing the sacrosanct America's Cup and saying cheekily, 'If people ask where Australia is, tell them that's where the America's Cup is.' This second commercial was launched in, of all places, that bastion of American yachting, the New York Yacht Club itself, which says something for the Americans' ability to forgive and forget. At first, the club committee hadn't been too keen on inviting a singleted Hogan into the august purlieus of their premises. But on being assured that Paul would be 'decently' garbed, they gave in.

On the day, Paul arrived looking very respectable, actually sporting what he described as 'this unnatural piece of equipment' (i.e., a tie), which did something to disguise the fact that the top button of his shirt wasn't done up. Noticing that workmen were digging up the sidewalk outside the Club, just off Fifth Avenue, Paul ad libbed: 'G'day. First thing I'd like to do is thank the New York Yacht Club. If there's one thing I really like, it's a gracious loser. We got the Cup and the bolts and when I come here today I see you've started to dig up the whole foundations. I was moved almost to tears.' Certain committee members looked somewhat granite-faced at this. Nevertheless they graciously hosted a reception in a marble-floored room and then a luncheon upstairs.

In New York, where his first commercial had only just been screened, Paul found the same kind of enthusiastic response he had received on the West Coast. After being – on first acquaintance – mistaken for someone from Austria, expected to yodel, Paul found New Yorkers grappling with the vowel-twisting of 'G'day.' He was surprised to discover that he was recognized on the sidewalks of New York. After having his hand almost shaken off, he remarked, 'The more I walk around the United States, the more I see you buggers need a holiday.' Three thousand callers a day seemed to agree after the East Coast saw the ad. MoJo won a US advertising award for their efforts – third prize in the multi-media advertising awards in New York for 1984, and Madison Avenue's advertising heavyweights were fulsome in their praise of the campaign. Paul was on the way to becoming a cult figure to more than just a handful of Los Angeles restaurant-goers.

Invited to appear on the Johnny Carson Show, he turned the opportunity down when he was told he had to rehearse his act. He said he preferred to ad lib. (Later he did agree to appear.) The top-rated US show *60 Minutes* interviewed him. Introducing him as Australia's answer to Monty Python, interviewer Dianne Sawyer probed him on why he had satirized the clothing warn by religious leaders. Paul stood up for himself, saying that the Pope, sitting as he did on God's right hand, was big enough to take some light satire. He told the interviewer he thought some Americans were too serious, and then just went into overdrive and did a straight Hoges act. The interviewer also probed about Australia's convict origins. Paul came up with a good reply: 'We were convicts. You lot got away. The ones that escaped went to America, and those of us who weren't quick enough off the mark were sent in convict ships out to Australia. We are partners in crime, we were the rabble and no-hopers, not so much criminals but people who bucked the system.'

It didn't take Foster's long to take advantage of Paul's success in America. In 1985 they decided to launch a sales drive in Canada under a licensing agreement with the Canadian brewer, Carling O'Keefe Ltd. The Canadian campaign was an interesting variation on the UK one. Again much of the credit for its subsequent success must go to Paul himself for finding the right wavelength. With the help of the J. Walter Thompson agency, Paul pitched his appeal perfectly, combining a rare comprehension of what Canadians are interested in with a cheeky mockery of that same thing.

Usually, as Canadian commentators said, Canadians are very sensitive to being the butt of 'dumb northerner'' jokes. But Paul, with the help of the Toronto office of JWT, pulled off a sly Aussie coup. In one ad, Paul, dressed casually, wanders through a fancy garden party. 'G'day,' he begins, and then goes into a line of patter about the similarities between Canada and Oz. He refers to 'roughing it under canvas', i.e., dining in elegance under a garden marquee, and 'cooking over an open fire' – barbecuing with all luxury conveniences – and then he tells Canadians how lucky they are to have the old Foster's 'to make it all bearable.' Then, in like Flynn,* Paul does his pitch. Sidling up to an exquisitely dressed woman wearing a mink stole, Paul says, 'They're selling the liquid gold for the price of your regular brew.' He gives the woman and the stole an appreciative glance, then arches his eyebrows and adds, 'Just as well, too. Looks like some of youse (sic) still has to go out and trap your own coats.'

It went down well. One journalist working in Toronto reported, 'Canadians love it, possibly because it's such a contrast to the sanctimonious ignorance that others – the Americans and British in particular – show towards Canada. Canadians seem to feel a certain kinship with Australia that Hogan plays on. The hard part is grasping Hogan's version of the English language, but it seems to have become an acquired taste. In fact, the Foster's ads are often more entertaining than the cops-and-robbers shows that surround them. Possibly because Hogan needs to be listened to carefully, his ads bring many living rooms to silence and attentiveness.' The campaign proved to be a success and led the Australian Tourist Commission to decide to launch its own Hogan ads in Canada in early 1987.

Given this success, Foster's decided it was time to take on the huge American market. (Actually they had tried before, to the extent of having 27 July 1984, declared 'Foster's Lager Day' in the City of Los Angeles. But the impact of the earlier campaign had apparently been minimal, for Foster's was languishing way, way down the list of more than 400 beers imported into the US.) The new Hogan campaign launch date was set for 1 May 1986, and they chose again to start with the West Coast market, despite the fact that America's East Coast had traditionally been the best place to sell imported beers – because of the German and other European backgrounds of many people in the Eastern states. Foster's sent out a news release, praising Paul and beating their own drum about their long association with him, first through his UK Foster's commercials, then in the series made for Canada, and finally in the USA. To kick off the USA Foster's TV campaign, Paul flew over to be guest-of-honour at a barbecue at the Los Angeles home of the Australian Consul-General, where a firm called Barbeques Galore flew in 10,000 prawns and sacrified several lambs for a bash attended by 600 of LA's high society. Next Paul was invited to a ceremony in LA where he was presented with a certificate signed by the Mayor of Los Angeles, Tom Bradley, proclaiming Wednesday, 30 April 1986 'Paul Hogan Day' in the City of Los Angeles (apparently they'll do anything to help outsiders in that friendly city).

The proclamation read:

CITY OF LOS ANGELES
PROCLAMATION
PAUL HOGAN DAY

Whereas Paul Hogan has become a familiar face to the people of the United States as the ambassador of goodwill from Australia (Down Under), who has promised to 'put another shrimp on the barbie' for us in his Australian tourism television commercials; and

Whereas Paul Hogan will presently embark upon a new television advertising campaign in the United States for Australia's largest brewery, Carlton and United, maker of Australia's most successful beer export, Foster's Lager; and

Whereas Paul Hogan's work on behalf of Foster's Lager
has already and will continue to help employ
thousands of Los Angelenos; and
Whereas Los Angeles seeks always to further and enrich its
feeling of friendship with the people of Australia;
Now, Therefore, I, Tom Bradley, Mayor of the City of Los
Angeles, do hereby proclaim April 30, 1986, 'Paul
Hogan Day' in Los Angeles and on behalf of our
three million citizens extend our warmest
welcome to Mr Hogan.

Dated: April 30, 1986   Signed: *Tom Bradley*, Mayor.

With characteristic cheek, Paul told the guests at the
ceremony at the Regency Hyatt Hotel – where genuine
Aussie meat pies and tinnies of Foster's were served to 40
guests who included the Australian Consul-General – that
he'd been expecting to be given the keys to the city. 'Getting
the keys to a city means you can do anything you like and not
get arrested,' he grinned. 'I was planning one hell'uva day,
but I'll accept this proclamation anyway.' He was feeling
particularly cocky that day, for he'd just heard that *Crocodile
Dundee* had out-grossed *E.T.* and *Rocky IV* by bringing in
A$1.8-million in its first week in Australia. 'It's great to
knock them off,' he said, swigging a beer. 'Now we're
thinking of doing another one. It might be a sequel.' But that
was to be a while off yet.

Interestingly, the US Foster's commercials, created by
another Sydney ad agency, George Patterson, had a theme
not dissimilar to that of *Crocodile Dundee* – that of an Australian innocent from the backwoods who visits America, mou-
thing Ockerisms like 'g'day' and trying to understand
typical American pastimes. One commercial was a send-up
of Miller Lite TV ads; another showed Paul fishing for trout

and a third showed Paul being confused by frisbee throwing, which he described as 'chucking your plates around after lunch.' The USA firm which imported Foster's, All Brand Importers, were quick to describe the resemblance between the film and the commercials as purely 'coincidence', and added that the commercials were made first. However, they saw the potential of the movie and planned their autumn media purchases of commercial space to coincide with the opening of *Crocodile Dundee* city-by-city. All Brand Importers was later able to announce that sales of Foster's had shot up 14 per cent by the end of 1986. Another, perhaps rather less reliable analysis said that sales had soared 1600 per cent!

There was no doubt that, one way and another, Paul Hogan was beginning to become almost a household name – or at least face – in America. By November 1985 visa applications for Australia had increased 85 per cent on the previous year, and the momentum of tourists making the decision to take a holiday in the land of Wonder Down Under was steadily increasing. Yet while things were going just fine for Foster's and Australian tourism in America, South Africa banned Paul's ads from its TV screens on the grounds that his utterances of such watered-down expletives as 'Strewth' were blasphemous. The South African Broadcasting Company's TV advertising department rejected seven of the 12 ads. Meanwhile, Canada had come back for another taste of Hogan – this time a modified version of his Australian tourism ads.

Meanwhile, in Australia, it was announced that Paul had been chosen as the 1986 Australian of the Year in recognition of his services to Australian tourism and, indeed, to Australian culture and the entertainment industry generally. It was an honour that was long overdue. In the same week (the reason being that Australia Day, 26 January, is the occasion for such honours) it was announced from Canberra that Paul had been awarded membership of the prestigious Order of Australia. That was not the end of the good news that week. Within a day or so Paul learned that, at 43, he had become a proud grandfather. Paul, unfortunately, was unable to accept his Australian of the Year award in person – he was in Canada shooting a Foster's commercial at the time – but, to his surprise, his son Brett offered to accept the award on his behalf. Paul had always thought his kids tried to avoid the limelight. When presenting the award to Brett, the Chairman of the National Australia Day Council, tennis star John Newcombe, praised Paul for having 'personally affected the lives of so many Australians without any benefits to himself.'

On a freezing winter's day in Canada in early 1987, as the country shivered under particularly bitter temperatures, Paul arrived to try to coax what the Australian Tourist Commission hoped would be 70,000 Canadians to visit Australia by the bicentennial year of 1988 (marking the 200th anniversary, celebrated on 26 January, of the founding of the first white settlement in Australia). By this time Hogan's name was doubly famous in Canada because *Crocodile Dundee* had been released, augmenting the impact of the Foster's and Tourist Commission ads. The film was to do particularly well in Canada, eventually accounting for more than 13 per cent of its North American gross – in a country with only 9 per cent of the North American continent's population. Launching the tourism ads, Alan Drew of the ATC said he wasn't worried that they might look like pale adaptations of either the Foster's commercials or *Crocodile Dundee*. 'In fact, the reverse,' he said. 'Foster's will gain from the fact that Hogan is seen in the marketplace in another light, and we will gain from the fact that Paul is also on the Foster's ad and in *Crocodile Dundee*.'

But we are beginning to get too far ahead of our story. The advertisements Paul had done, first for Winfield, next for Foster's and then for the Australian Tourist Commission, helped set up a situation that allowed Paul to put into effect an ambition he and John Cornell had held for more than a decade. With Paul's name and face well-known not only in Australia but now in North America and Britain, it was time to take the last big step – towards Tinseltown.

INTERVAL

Creature Feature

MANY PEOPLE who have never ventured to Australia might be under the misapprehension that the famous crocodile attack scene in *Crocodile Dundee*, in which the lovely Linda Kozlowski is grabbed by a fearsome-looking croc, is a case of Hogan and his film-making mates, to use an Australianism, 'coming the raw prawn' (in other words, having you on). Not so. It would be a serious mistake for foreigners to Australia's otherwise hospitable shores to imagine that what one local poet called 'this sunburnt country, this wide brown land' is a totally congenial, innocuous place populated by happy aborigines (at least that part's right, so long as you avoid late-night bars in Sydney's King's Cross), cute little koala bears, hippity-hopping kangaroos and wallabies and little furry marsupials like the duck-billed platypus – surely the world's oddest animal – and various possums, wombats and bandicoots who wouldn't say boo to a fly, let alone a tourist. A recent headline in the New York *Post* should be enough to dispel this dangerous ignorance. It read:

AMERICAN MODEL EATEN ALIVE BY KILLER CROC

D. H. Lawence remarked in his little-read but uncannily perceptive 1922 Australian novel *Kangaroo* (made recently into another film from Down Under), that the largest flesh-eating predator in Australia is the dingo, an animal made famous by a recent incident when a baby was allegedly abducted and consumed by this remote relative to the common or garden pooch (and to be the subject of yet another Oz film). But Lawrence was referring only to purely land-based creatures. If you take the water into account, there are some rather more substantial carnivores lurking there which the unwary visitor should be warned about. Putting crocs aside for the moment, probably the most dangerous are the numerous species of shark that populate the beaches and rivers, especially in warmer waters. Some of these, such as the fetchingly nicknamed Great White Death, make even the clockwork monster in the film *Jaws* look anaemic (though perhaps the most ferocious is an unpleasant mid-sized variety called the bronzed whaler which enjoys harassing swimmers in estuaries). To relieve excessive fears, however, it should be noted that since Australia started meshing (netting) sharks off the main swimming beaches there hasn't been a fatal or serious shark attack in living memory.

Yet the nastiest of God's creatures in Australia are not great but small. The deadliest, gram to gram, is probably the sea wasp, a kind of jellyfish first brought to public attention by Conan Doyle's chilling Sherlock Holmes story, 'The Lion's Tail'. The sea wasp's sting is fatal, full stop. It drifts around off many of the northern coasts, obliging otherwise macho Aussie male surfers to wear panty-hose in infested waters, a sight that some overseas visitors have misinterpreted and from which unfortunate misunderstandings have subsequently ensued. Equally terminal is the sting of the blue-ringed octopus, a denizen of coastal rock pools. Its bite is poisonous enough to kill ten men.

The water has other hazards, too. On the beautiful Great Barrier Reef and in other tropical shallows one must be very careful where one puts one's foot, for there hides the dreaded stone fish, so called because it looks to the casual eye like a piece of innocent rock or coral. But its spines are poisonous and an unshod foot carelessly planted thereon will require immediate and painful hospitalization. There are also the several varieties of sea snakes: brilliant green, yellow and pink creatures which swish through the water like waving ribbons. Their bite can also be fatal. Fortunately they again prefer the regions north of the Tropic of Capricorn where, for this and many other reasons, swimming is discouraged.

On shore the kin of these snakes are only marginally less deadly. Avoid, for example, the red-bellied black snake and the aptly-named tiger snake – indeed, all reptiles of the slithery kind. Walking through the bush without proper foot protection is asking for trouble, especially in cane-growing regions where the terrible taipan dwells. Then there are the spiders, some of which are unique to Australia – which is fortunate for other places. Most feared is the funnel-web, probably the most murderous of the species *arachnida*. Its favourite haunts are the environs of many Sydney suburban homes, either in the clay outside or the shoe cupboard inside. The funnel-web has a close relative, the fairly deadly trap-door spider, which has a disconcerting habit of jumping out of its burrow and biting passing animals. Yet perhaps the spider to be most wary of is the tiny red-back whose purlieu is the dark recesses of outhouses, especially that useful exterior facility Australians call a dunny.

This does not exhaust the list of creatures to be avoided Down Under. There are also only occasionally fatal things like centipedes and just merely painful ones like bull ants, blue-bottles (another sort of jellyfish) and sea lice, the latter a more southerly cousin of the sea wasp. Ticks, which burrow into the necks of children and dogs, should especially be eschewed. Also be wary of leeches in creeks and billabongs, and if possible avoid such comparatively benign annoyances as mosquitoes, bees and the innumerable types of fly (see appendix).

Apart from the dingo – which is enjoying a certain contemporary vogue, at least in juvenile circles – there is no doubt that the Australian creature most people currently fear is the crocodile, and not only because of the publicity afforded it by Mick Dundee. That American model who was taken so luridly by a crocodile in Australia's Gulf country was only one of an increasing number of victims of croc attacks in recent years. Just on a year before, in February 1986, there was an almost identical incident in which a 31-year-old fishing hand, Katie McQuarrie, was taken and killed by a 20-foot-plus croc while she was wading out to a boat. (So shocked were the locals that profits from the weekly two-up* game in the local hotel, the Animal Bar, were donated to a fund set up by the unfortunate girl's family. Her boyfriend, who was with her when the attack occurred, was commendably laconic about the event. 'I don't blame the croc,' he was quoted as saying.)

And only a month before that another 31-year-old woman, Beryl Wruck, was seized as she cooled off in shallow water after a party. (Her body was later found inside the guilty croc.) About a year earlier another lady, Val Plumwood, 39, was mauled by a croc in the Northern Territory. She somehow managed to escape its clutches by climbing a nearby tree, but the croc followed her up and pulled her down again. Finally she managed to fight it off, then crawled more than a mile for help. 'The scarring has created problems for me,' she said later, 'especially in my feelings for my body.' But this did not disillusion Ms Plumwood, who harbours nothing but admiration for the creatures even though, as she says, 'not many have had their opinions as strongly tested as me.'

Since 1870 there have been 53 fatal crocodile attacks recorded in Australia. Ominously, more than a third of these have happened in the past six years. The culprit is the *crocodylus porosus* or estuarine crocodile which attains a length of more than 20 feet and can live more than 100 years. Its habitat is the salt-water precincts near the mouths and lower reaches of Australian and South-East Asian rivers. One of the oldest surviving species on Earth (it has remained largely unchanged for 200 million years), it lives on fish and whatever it can grab that comes within jaw range. It usually drowns its larger prey and stores it until tender, having no grinding molars for tougher food. It is pretty quick underwater and even on land can notch up a creditable 10 mph gallop when it feels the need to scurry.

The probable reason for the croc's higher profile in recent years is the fact that since 1972 it has been a protected species in Australia (which makes what Mr Dundee supposedly did for a living shamefully illegal). Before that it was unmercifully exploited, the croc being regarded as one of nature's baddies. But when it became clear that such prejudice had brought it to the verge of extinction, it was rehabilitated, and shooting, skinning and selling its skin for shoes and handbags became a crime. Unfortunately, the croc has proved singularly ungrateful for this vote of confidence and has taken advantage of the respite to develop an appetite for human flesh.

From perhaps 2000 adult crocs (the figure is widely disputed) in 1972, they have proliferated to something like 20,000 or perhaps even 100,000 today. Worse, the smaller crocs, which hitherto had been heavily culled, were able to grow into bigger crocs, at the rate of about a foot a year. As a big croc needs more food than a small one, and the food supply remained unchanged except that more and more humans invaded croc territory – mainly to fish, catch prawns and observe the ever-lengthening crocodiles – the reptiles' attention switched more and more to what was readily available, namely people. 'They're getting pretty spoiled,' said one old croc-hunter, 'and cheeky with it. They think man's not their enemy any more but rather a source of food. They're beginning to make a real nuisance of themselves. Soon they'll be killing people left, right and centre.'

A living example of how cheeky they can get is Alf Casey, a Queensland cane farmer who had a pet croc in his backyard for a number of years. Then one day Alf, 69, made a grievous error which cost him the lower half of his left arm. 'It was my own stupid fault,' he said later. 'I said the word fish – a word she knows – and I didn't have one ready for her. She bit off my arm by mistake. It definitely wasn't her fault. It's just one of those things.' Alf was in hospital 19 days and refused all pleas, particularly from his 63-year-old wife Rae, to have the croc, Charlene, 23, destroyed. But every cloud has a silver lining. When the film was being promoted Alf and Rae were invited over to the States on a croc promotional tour, appearing on various talk shows to explain how he came to have one arm shorter than the other.

The curious thing about all this is the way the survivors of crocodile attacks seem anxious not to attach any blame to the crocs. Unlike sharks, snakes, spiders and other notorious Australian killers, the croc enjoys a good press. Indeed, they have become a major tourist atraction, for which the film is only partly responsible. The Japanese in particular are flocking to the croc-infested areas and pay large sums to be taken to where they might observe the creatures. Americans, too, regard a trip to croc country as almost an obligatory stop on the trip Down Under, like seeing the Opera House and the Sydney Harbour Bridge. (A recent party from the States got more than they bargained for when they inadvertently observed a fisherman being taken by a croc on one of their tours.) One visitor from a southern Australian State was overheard to remark during another croc country package tour: 'Wow! So this is the place people actually get eaten by crocodiles!' For those less intrepid, the croc enclosures at Australian city zoos are proving a riveting attraction. Most of the crocs here, however, are of a different breed, the smaller fresh-water croc or *crocodylus johnstoni* which is almost a vegetarian.

Australians, being the entrepreneurial race they are, haven't been backward in trying to cash in on the croc vogue. Already crocs have featured prominently in two recent locally-made productions, the TV mini-series *Return to Eden* (in which the heroine is mauled by a croc) and the film *Burke and Wills*. Outside the National Australia Bank in Gymea, New South Wales, the manager, Warren Nalty, has installed a large fish tank containing a live croc. The attached sign says: 'Put the bite on us for a personal loan.' And the tourist potential is being ruthlessly milked. Up in Jabiru in the Gulf country they're building a new $13 million hotel in the shape of a giant croc. It's over 250 metres long and, as the architect says: 'From the air it looks like it just crawled out of the lake.' It's expected to be a big attraction, especially for the Japanese. Also croc farms producing crocodile steaks for the table are beginning to spring up all over the North. Qantas, Australia's national airline, is even rumoured to be serving fresh croc on its first-class flights across the Pacific. Crocodile is supposed to taste a bit like veal, but with the texture of lobster, and costs about $20 a pound. 'It's great with noodles or soy sauce,' said one farmer, with perhaps an eye to the sushi market.

However, lest the intending tourist be put off by either the threat of the croc and its many deadly colleagues in Australia or by the apparent flippancy with which the native Australians seem to treat the subject, a word of reassurance should be added. The chance of encountering a croc or any other predator in Australia is so remote it can be safely dismissed (so long as one follows the advice of tour guides and knowledgeable – rather than smart-alec – locals). Australia is a big place – as big as America – and its 15 million or so souls rattle round fairly comfortably in the vast empty spaces. And the often macabre Australian sense of humour, particularly when it is good-naturedly applied to visitors, should always be taken into account. Still, it would be prudent not to go swimming in croc waters, and remember to take a spare pair of panty-hose, just in case.

CHAPTER 8

From Tinnies to Tinseltown

For a personality like Hogan not to make his first feature film until more than 15 years after his TV debut is a phenomenon that is little short of amazing. Since 1972 literally thousands of Australian films have been made – a few excellent, some so-so and the rest pretty ghastly – employing every Tom, Dick and Bruce in the Australian entertainment scene and beyond. Some of the outside personalities who have made Australian movies include stars like Dennis Hopper (*Mad Dog Morgan*), Mick Jagger (*Ned Kelly*) and Kirk Douglas (he played not one but two roles in *The Man from Snowy River*) before Australia's actors' union, Equity, derailed the gravy train and clamped down on the employment of foreign actors in Australian films.

It wasn't that Hogan lacked for movie offers. Indeed, on his own count he turned down at least 60 movie parts in those 15 or so years. One early one had been the starring and largely naked role in *Alvin Purple*, a vulgar sex romp. Paul said no. It turned out to be mildly successful. This didn't faze Paul. He had never felt that he'd be comfortable taking off his clothes in public. Other parts he turned down included a big role in *Don's Party*, a film about a group of people having a party on the eve of the election of Gough Whitlam in 1972 when the Labor Party took power after 25 years in the political wilderness. This film was also mildly successful, at least in Australia. Each time Paul said 'no' it was partly because he genuinely didn't feel he could agree to nudity or bad language in the movies, he had always been innately conservative about such things. 'Also we didn't want to throw Paul away on something that wasn't good and wasn't funny,' said manager Cornell. 'We've knocked back some of the worst films ever made in Australia.' Paul commented, 'Most of the scripts we knocked back were not comedies and the ones that were, weren't funny. None of them were right, and eventually the penny dropped that if I was going to get the right one, I'd have to write it myself.'

Yet Paul was not a total movie virgin by the time he appeared in *Crocodile Dundee*. And he finally got the chance to get some movie experience without having to write his own script. An offer to appear in a film-for-television series being shot in September–October 1985 for Australia's Nine Network appealed to him and Cornell. The plot of the A\$6.5 million mini-series, *Anzacs*, centred on the business acumen of a smart young Aussie soldier in World War I who could see a few quid in the nefarious activities of a certain lady called Madame who ran a mobile hotel not far from the mud-filled trenches. The opportunity to appear in the mini-series was attractive for a number of reasons. It would give Paul invaluable experience in the technique of film, as distinct from television. It would help to broaden his TV-commercial image. And, above all, it would present him for the first time as a straight actor – and, incidentally, as the beginnings of a sex symbol.

Paul warmed to the idea of playing the role of a larrikin

Aussie, Pat Cleary, fighting the Hun in the First World War, who is conned into thinking that Marie, the beautiful young daughter of the local madam, known as Madame, was enamoured of him. The plot turns on Pat being lured into a secret midnight tryst with the daughter, only to find Madame waiting for him. Paul liked the down-to-earth Australian characteristics of the hero and agreed to play the role. Although he doesn't appear nude, he can be seen revealing more of his muscular torso than ever before on camera in a bedroom scene with the earthy Frenchwoman, Madame, played by Australian actress Elaine Lee, former star of the TV soap 'Number 99'. Although he gets to slip between Madame's sheets, it is really a mutual business deal that interests them both.

Having agreed to play the role of the Aussie digger, Paul then set off for a whistlestop tour of the East Coast of America to promote his Australian tourism commercials. Although his real movie debut was yet to come, he was already a celebrity on the West Coast. Now it was the turn of the rest of America to see Paul Hogan slip a shrimp on the barbie. The publicity campaign was well-planned. In the two weeks he was in the USA, Paul guested on more than 40 talk shows, including the prestigious Merv Griffin Show. Day-in, day-out, he smiled his charming, cheeky grin, telling his story over and over. 'You'd think I was up for election for President, the number of places I had to turn up,' he said. Interestingly, he also began getting numerous offers of TV and movie roles. Some were in pilot films, others offers to star in his own series. Some were in already-established series. Paul returned to Australia for the shooting of *Anzacs*, leaving Cornell behind to sort out the offers. Some were from big studios and networks – ABC, NBC, Warner Bros and Disney. Paul confessed to being mystified at the reaction his TV commercials had produced: 'I'm still scratching my head over it.' He wasn't yet ready to plunge into the American TV or movie scene.

Returning to Australia, he began work on location for *Anzacs*. As he grew into the role he realized that it was tailor-made for him. He was allowed to write some of his own dialogue, which helped him sound all the more natural. Pat, whom Paul described as 'a chook raffler gone to war', could easily have been Paul's real-life grandfather, volunteering to fight on the Western Front and at Gallipoli. George Miller, a leading Australian film-maker, who helped make *The Man from Snowy River* such a movie success, was one of the directors on *Anzacs*. Before they began shooting, he did a series of readings with Paul. 'He's going to be brilliant,' George enthused. 'His character is a real larrikin – irreverent, shameless, humorous and irrepressible.' The series producer, Geoff Burrows, later said: 'As the character of Pat Cleary developed during the series it became evident that not only could Paul play the character, but also he *was* the character – something that would become more apparent in *Crocodile Dundee*. Like Paul in real life, Pat had tried his hand at plenty of jobs before volunteering to go to World War I, inadvertently becoming a hero.

Although the series had a large cast, with 25 main lead actors, Paul was singled out by the press and the critics as the real star. He was beginning to demonstrate that he possessed true star-power – and sex appeal. His masculinity, muscular biceps, and seemingly innocent blue eyes all added up to potential film stardom. Looking every inch the bronzed digger, Paul, in a slouch hat tilted irreverently on the back of his head, his webbings in a mess, wandered round the south side of Phillip Island, near Melbourne, which had been turned into Anzac Cove at Gallipoli, munching enormous sandwiches. He was, he mumbled, 'doin' my bit for Australia.' 'It's not like playing Othello,' he said.

'It's really no great challenge.' On location his co-stars teased him for getting all the perks – like two sandwiches instead of one. He'd retort that it wasn't two but three. 'I'm the star, mate,' he'd say. 'I even get my own little make-up sheila.'

An unspoken conviction started to develop during the making of *Anzacs* that somehow Paul Hogan, TV comic and beer and cigarette commercial personality, had moved up into a new league. Paul found making *Anzacs* a doddle. He'd based some of the character on his Nasho* experience and his ten years as a part-time volunteer in the CMF (Citizens Military Forces), where he rose to 'the dizzying heights of corporal'. He added, 'Making movies is a bit like being in the army.' Despite having to film much of the series in mud on location in Melbourne, Paul enjoyed the 20 weeks of filming *Anzacs*. It was a change from the more hectic round of making his Paul Hogan shows:

'You've got more time – you don't have to compromise. With television there's always the budget you've got to keep within. If you want to do Custer's Last Stand in a sketch, you do it with three or four Indians. You do that in a film, you get in 3000! Instead of being the producer, writer, assistant director, coffee maker, budget watcher, accountant and doing all that I normally do with a Hogan Show, I just sort of wander on to the set here, do my lines, wander off and wait for the next scene.' Paul was getting the taste for film-making. And he added enigmatically that after *Anzacs* he planned one more TV comedy special, 'but from the middle of next year I'm tied up for the following year with other things.'

The reason he'd be tied up was *Crocodile Dundee*. The moment had come for him to switch from advertising cans of Foster's and boosting Australia to making his first feature film. He would indeed be trying to graduate from tinnies to Tinseltown. The idea for the film grew from a number of different seeds. One was an interview Paul had seen years back on Australian TV when the English chat show star, Michael Parkinson, had been doing a guest series in Sydney and had interviewed a bloke from the Northern Territory, a crocodile hunter who had been savaged by one of these untrustworthy beasts. Paul was intrigued by the image of the croc hunter and what he'd gone through – and the fact that, being an innocent from the Bush, he didn't even know who Michael Parkinson was. Another seed was his experiences when he'd first gone to New York. Even though Sydney is hardly a hick town, Manhattan took him by surprise. He had only been in New York briefly, doing the talk shows, but he soon realized that he was regarded like a creature from outer space with his strange accent. 'It was like I came from the moon! I thought, if they think *I'm* alien, if they got hold of some of the outback characters I've met and put them into that whole scene over there, it'd be like the War of the Worlds.'

Paul began toying with the idea of creating his own heroic Australian character rather than doing what most of the other Australian movie-makers had done in the past, basing their films on a real character from history such as the evil Breaker Morant or the bushranger Ned Kelly. Paul always envisaged his character, Mick, as being a very dry, self-contained bushman, to whom time didn't mean a thing. 'That nice, slow "she'll be right" quality you find in the Australian outback people,' is how Paul put it. He outlined the character to Cornell around 1984 and they began working on the idea. 'The first thing we decided was that it should be entertaining,' Cornell said later. 'We didn't want to frighten the audience, or bore them shitless or teach them anything or push our philosophy or politics at them. . . . A lot of Australian films have been very good but few of them have been as entertaining, perhaps, as they should have been.' After a research trip to croc country in the Northern Territory, where Paul also observed the tough dynamite fishermen of the Gulf, the plot began to take shape. 'There are a few outlaws up there,' he said. 'I like them – there's something very Australian about them.

Paul and Ken Shadie, his trusted *Paul Hogan Show* writer, began working on a script. Paul would scribble down his ideas with a pencil (because he can't type) and Shadie would pull it all together in a draft script. Cornell acted as script editor. Finally, after the sixth draft, they felt they had the makings of a movie. The headquarters of their JP Productions (Paul's and Cornell's private company – they formed a separate company, Rimfire Films, to actually do the movie) was an unglamorous office down a back lane in the inner Sydney suburb of Camperdown. They worked on the script and tried out possible outfits for Mick Dundee to wear. Paul kept a close eye on every detail. When a black cowboy hat was tried on him, he wondered whether it might throw too heavy a shadow on his face. A smaller-brimmed hat was the eventual answer. Paul was confident that the film would find a market outside Australia for the romantic bushman character. 'And I'm seen as an Australian type acceptable both in Europe and America. I know what they laugh at in Spain or Surrey, and for Americans, we've got New York.' When the shooting script was finally finished, much of it was Paul's own work.

Next they had to raise the necessary cash. They reckoned they'd need around US$6 million: chicken-feed compared with most movie budgets. They had no trouble raising the money; their mates like cricketers Greg Chappell, Rodney Marsh and Dennis Lillee put money into it, and there were other, smaller investors – indeed, they had to knock back around $3 million because they didn't think they'd need it. Unlike most Australian film-makers, they didn't ask for a single dollar of Government funding. Cornell and Paul put in half the money themselves (their share of 50 per cent of the profits would be split two-thirds to Hogan and one-third to Cornell). The Brisbane stockbroker Paul Morgan and Co underwrote the film without pre-sales. The film's prospectus stated that A$450,000 had been allocated for the principal artist (Paul Hogan). Director Faiman was to get A$160,000. The story and script fee for Hogan and Shadie, was A$218,000. Producer's fee (Cornell and the line producer, Jane Scott) would get A$315,000. Once the money was lined up the film was definitely a 'goer'.

Paul said that his decision to play the lead role as Mick J. Dundee was obvious: 'Can't think of anyone better to play him.' By June 1985 a highly professional Australian film crew had been hired, including cinematographer Russell Boyd, whose track record included *Gallipoli*, *Mrs Boffel*, *Picnic at Hanging Rock* and *Year of Living Dangerously*. Also most of the cast had been chosen, including the comic character actor John Meillon. It would be his 36th film since *On the Beach* in 1953. He explained that the part of Mick Dundee's business partner in Never Never Safaris ('It's called that because if you go on one, you'll never, never come back') was based loosely on a character he'd played years before in the early TV comedy *My Name's McGooly*. Another member of the cast was the aboriginal actor, David Gulpilil, who would play the role of Mick Dundee's childhood mate. The 13-week shoot in the Northern Territory and north-west Queensland would begin in July 1985, then would move to New York in September.

Hogan promised that the movie would be good for Australia's image. It wouldn't be a 'Jaws on legs' nor a 'search for the golden boomerang.' Neatly summing up the plot, he said: 'It's an Aussie tale of romance, comedy and adventure. The lead character is a knockabout Aussie bloke. He meets an American bird in the Northern Territory and they go to New York together.' Asked if the movie would be anything like *Bazza Mackenzie* (the earlier Australian movie starring Barry Humphries' innocent abroad in London), Paul snorted: 'Bazza was obsessed with bodily functions. He was an idiot, an Australian fool for the English to laugh at. My character, Crocodile Dundee, is a horse of a different colour. He doesn't make a fool of himself wherever he goes and he's not obsessed with pointing Percy at the porcelain. Dundee may be naive and a larrikin but he's no fool. He'd chew Bazza up and spit him out before brekky.'

Paul also emphasised that *Crocodile Dundee* was different from most other recent Australian movies – if he had audiences in tears, it would be from laughing. And the hero would still be alive when the credits rolled. 'The hero dies in the ones that have had any success, like *Gallipoli* and *Breaker Morant*,' he said. 'Even in *Phar Lap* the horse died in the end. We haven't got a great tradition of comedy.'

Cornell refused to pre-sell the movie abroad (the main way Australian film-makers had hitherto helped to finance their movies, apart from Government grants), believing that pre-sales tended to restrict a moviemaker. He also thought that he would probably get a better price if he waited till he had some footage to show the major distributors. But he did strike early on what is believed to have been a very good deal with the Australian cinema chain of Hoyts. The sum was not disclosed but is said to have been the highest ever paid for an Australian movie. The deal was struck with the then Hoyts managing director, Terry Jackman, who later became the film's sales consultant. The plan was to screen the movie the following April (1986) simultaneously in 75 cinemas – a record for Australia.

But before they even started shooting, one considerable hurdle they had to face was to find the right actress to play the American TV reporter. Getting the Australian branch of Actors' Equity to agree to an American actress playing the role of the American news reporter proved a serious problem. Despite the fact that both Paul and Cornell were card-carrying members of Equity, the union dug in its heels, claiming that the part should go to a battling Aussie who might fake a New York accent – a solecism almost equivalent to an Australian playing D. H. Lawrence in the film *Kangaroo*. Paul felt strongly on the matter: 'You'll always get people saying we could get an Australian girl to do an American accent – they do it real good. They don't. Phoney accents are something I hate with a passion, anyway. I hate to see Pommie guys turning up on M.A.S.H. as Australians. It makes me want to throw up.' Paul and Cornell asked for a chance to put their case to Equity's policy committee, but were turned down. They next approached the Immigration Minister, Chris Hurford. Equity warned they'd fight to the bitter end. But curiously, when the time came for the hearing, Equity didn't turn up to make its case and the government had no choice but to let Linda Kozlowski, a New York actress who'd been personally recommended by Dustin Hoffman, with whom she'd played on the Broadway stage in *Death of a Salesman*, get the role.

The cameras were ready to roll. The main Australian scenes were to be shot in the Kakudu National Park in the Northern Territory, in Sydney and in a tiny hamlet in outback north-west Queensland called McKinlay – population 30. So into crocodile country the crew went, well-briefed on the dangers of that 200-million-year-old species. But the first location for shooting the film was the inland hamlet of McKinlay. With typical small-town suspicion, the locals weren't impressed by all this movie nonsense. The film team had taken over their town, knocking out the nice aluminium windows on the pub and splattering the freshly-painted walls of the police station with muck. Nevertheless, it was bringing money to the tiny town with its one main road lined with tired, paint-peeling buildings, a billiard saloon and a garage-cum-general store. Dumped down between Winton and Cloncurry in this godforsaken part of Queensland, McKinlay was not enjoying the fame of being Paul Hogan's re-creation of his childhood image of an Outback town like Lightning Ridge. The arrival of Hogan and his entourage, according to the locals, meant that the chooks* went crook.* The goats' milk dried up, too. They reckoned Paul Hogan was uppity and above himself, putting on airs as a movie star. Their beloved pub's name was summarily changed from the Federal Hotel to the Walkabout Creek Pub. In short, their normal, day-to-day lives had been disrupted. They even suspected they were being sent up – something to raise the hackles of any self-respecting Aussie.

'It's no credit to us that they chose McKinlay for their film,' said Jack Hardy, who had allowed his vacant shed to be turned into a bush garage for the film. 'They only came in here because the town was on its uppers.' One less-glum face was that of the local publican, Peter Ferris. The film crew had ordered in a lot of champagne and fancy wines. But then he got worried: there'd not be much call for that sort of grog once the team had moved on. Meanwhile he grinned and bore it, raking in the crew's money. Elsewhere, helicopters combed the area for aerial shots. Loudspeakers ordered people to move inside: they wanted a shot of an empty street. The locals had been told to park their cars in backyards and keep out of the action. A blonde stand-in for Linda Kozlowski had her moment of glory in the main street.

Then the shoot moved on to a new location, 70 km past

Cloncurry where Paul, Cornell and the team set up their canvas directors' chairs. Paul was seen in a tartan dressing-gown, partly to fend off the bitterly cold winter wind (July is winter in Australia), partly because Cornell didn't want his Crocodile Dundee gear to be prematurely exposed to the hovering photographers. One memorable moment on location was reported in the Sydney *Daily Mirror*: 'Hogan was following a tourist's car in his 4-wheel drive when the car in front stopped before fording a river. There was a sign which warned of saltwater crocs. To Hogan's astonishment the driver sent his wife out of the car to walk ahead up to her waist in water to ensure he could drive his vehicle safely to the other side. When Hogan had forded the river, he drew alongside the other driver and hollered angry abuse to him for risking his wife's life in the crocodile-infested river. The receiver of this tirade was about to rage back, then recognized who was giving him a blast, and became speechless.'

The scene in which the crocodile attacks Linda Kozlowski was shot at Girraween Lagoon, 30 km out of Darwin. The lagoon had previously been the location for the filming of *Return to Eden*, another crocodile saga, and *Burke and Wills*. Mike Atkinson, a Darwin cinematographer, hired for work on *Crocodile Dundee* because of his knowledge of the Australian bush, told Malcolm Brown of the *Sydney Morning Herald*: 'One of the main reasons (Girraween) was chosen was that there were no crocodiles there. It was an isolated lagoon cut off from tidal areas, so there was no risk to the crew.' The problem was, however, that the team wanted to make the attack look as real as possible. Could they use a real croc and tranquillize him so he wouldn't be dangerous? 'The insurance companies didn't like the idea,' Mike said. 'They said it wasn't foolproof. So in the end we had to build a mechanical croc and install it on a rail.' It took four months to construct the blood-curdlingly realistic six-metre-long, air-powered, latex fake crocodile – a master-piece of model-making.

Even early in the shooting schedule a feeling of confidence about the film was developing. Paul and Cornell had agreed that, unlike the TV show, Paul wouldn't be involved in the production side of the movie. Cornell told him, 'Just be Mick and don't worry about anything else,' Paul said. 'It was the only way to do it.' Paul had also insisted that there should be no prima donnas on the shoot. Initially Paul and Cornell were a little worried that maybe Linda wouldn't fit in with this egalitarian policy. 'Prima donnas, that's where money and time are wasted – running to the caravans and locking themselves in, refusing to come out because their hair is wrong or because they can't handle the scene. Linda was never like that. She was like us: "Go into the swamp, Linda. We'll keep the crocodiles away." "Okay". She just got on with the job. We never had to drag her out of the caravans.' And what about that kiss? In the film Paul gets his first screen kiss, despite the episode with Madame in *Anzacs*. 'We could've had a horrible debacle like Burt Lancaster and Deborah Kerr, rolling over together into the water.' He looked regretful for a moment. 'And to think I wrote the script!'

Linda enjoyed working with Paul, a man she found to be much more complicated than she had been led to believe. 'Paul has a real serious, contemplative, introspective side,' she said. She felt sceptical of his typical Aussie male 'no worries' act. While shooting out in crocodile country, she tried to get under his skin a little: 'I've said to Paul, "Come on, let's get real. You must worry." He denied it, saying "Nothing's that bad."' She found the pace gruelling but enjoyable. Paul had described her to the US magazine *People* as 'unemployed and broke. But she delivered the goods. She was a star in waiting. When she signed up and was coming to Australia, it worried us a little: she was a New Yorker. But she was terrific – a pleasure to work with. I don't think I could have done a love story with a bitch.'

Linda is grateful for the chance she got. At 28, she managed to skip a few rungs in the ladder of success, going from waitressing and the occasional stage role to international stardom in one swift leap. She also appreciated the feeling of being in on the creation of the film. Neither Paul nor Cornell had made a movie before. They were all in it together. And there were a lot of laughs – the sight of Paul grappling with the mechanical crocodile in the lagoon was one such occasion. As for Paul, well, said Cornell, it was much easier than doing the *Paul Hogan Show*, where Paul had to remember 40 pages of script at a go. With *Croc* he only had to remember one page at a time.

With the Australian shooting finished, it was on to New York for Mick Dundee's initiation into the Big Smoke. The Aussie crew found that they got on well with the American actors on the Manhattan leg of the shoot. The American cast included some of the best supporting actors in the country, such as Mark Blum (*Desperately Seeking Susan*), Michael Lombard (*Prizzi's Honor*), Ann Carlysle (*Liquid Sky* and *Desperately Seeking Susan*) and Irving Metzman (*Purple Rose of Cairo* and *Arthur*). And everywhere they set up for a shoot, passers-by, seeing in the flesh the man who slipped an extra shrimp on the barbie, rushed up to pump his hand and say 'G'day'.

'It was very heartening to find so many people interested in Australia,' Paul said. Scores of women would come up to him and tell him they wouldn't mind if he slipped a shrimp on to *their* barbie. Often they'd tell Paul he didn't look as tall in real life. This disconcerted him a bit: 'I'd always thought I was an average kind of height before – 175 cm. Now I feel like a jockey.' The crew swarmed over Manhattan, from the

Plaza Hotel to downtown Greenwich Village; they stopped the traffic on Fifth Avenue and took SoHo by storm. They were delighted, and more, with the results. 'We've done all we've come here to do, and more,' said Paul after he had completed a scene in which Mick Dundee and his female reporter friend are held up at knifepoint by muggers, and do more than just survive.

Paul was impressed by the way the New York City authorities bent over backwards to allow him and the crew the facilities they needed. 'New York makes filming as easy as pie,' he said, adding that he wished some of Australia's state authorities were as helpful. The five weeks of shooting, with one more to go in Sydney, had been a hard slog but Paul and Cornell were happy with what they'd achieved.

The only thing that interfered with the shooting schedule – and cost money in lost shooting time – was the hurricane forecast to hit Manhattan right in the middle of their shoot. And it wasn't just any old hurricane, but a real humdinger that was predicted. So serious was it expected to be that everybody was advised to retire to the basements of their buildings. It hit the headline news around the world: Manhattan shivered as the hurricane advanced. But in fact it turned out to be a wimp of a wind. The shooting time wasted cost $150,000 – but this was the only wasted time and money on the entire *Croc* budget. Paul said he felt right 'here' (touching his stomach) about the film. He promised it would be funny and entertaining and romantic. 'Yeh, there's romance. But it's romance in a subway in Brooklyn. It's real. Real romance doesn't take place in nice places anyway.'

Back home in Sydney for the post-production and the waiting, Paul took a close interest in the editing and sound recording. On one occasion he was able to make use of his experience as a boxer to suggest that a punch didn't sound quite right. A trial run of the movie was shown to a test audience in Los Angeles, and it was decided that for American audiences the early Australian part of the film should be shortened and certain ultra-Australianisms (such as 'stone the crows') which would be lost on the Americans should be omitted. As he waited for the premiere of the film in Australia, Paul confessed that it was the gamble of his life. It wasn't so much the dollars he had personally wagered on the movie, it was more his lifeblood and faith in himself and his judgement of what the movie audiences wanted. 'I've put everything I've worked for into it. If it doesn't work, I'm finished,' he said. 'If this film fails, then I've failed.'

Crocodile Dundee had its gala premiere in Australia on 25 April 1986. It was preceded by the usual previews for the local Press and critics. The response for the most part (there were some honourable exceptions) was lukewarm to downright rude. To explain this perversity, one has to remember here what the background history was. Ever since the early 1970s Australia had been churning out literally hundreds of home-grown films each year – at least if you count those film projects on which vast sums of taxpayers' money was expended in various sorts of film development grants. Most turned out to be A-1 turkeys, the majority not even making it to the actual release stage. Of those that did make it that far, most flopped immediately. A few had some sort of local success – though seldom returning the money spent making them – and some even went on to make an impression overseas. When, however, a list is made of these successes, only a comparative few titles can be recalled . . . *Picnic at Hanging Rock*, *Breaker Morant*, *My Brilliant Career*, *The Last Wave*, *Gallipoli*, *Caddie* and maybe a handful more. None of these, moreover, were great financial successes and none had general appeal to box office audiences, particularly outside Australia. Indeed, up until *Crocodile Dundee*'s premiere probably only one film (with sequels) had 'made it' overseas: *Mad Max*. And only one Australian star had become a big name outside home territory: Mel Gibson, the star of *Mad Max*.

The problem of lack of commercial successes had bedevilled the Australian film industry, artistically and economically, for years. With high hopes the best of what Australian film-makers produced would turn up each year at Cannes and other overseas launching pads, usually with a trailer-load of accompanying hype about The Great Australian Film, only to bomb out as soon as they got their cinema release. (Who remembers today *The Chant of Jimmy Black-smith*, which was supposed to conquer Cannes and the world back in the late 1970s?) The result was that by now most Australians had become reconciled to the fact that – *Mad Max* apart – the best the Australian film industry could hope for was some sort of critical success and low-yielding 'art' cinema releases. Then along came *Crocodile Dundee*. Not an art film, not a kooky film like *Mad Max*, but one unflin-chingly directed at the general cinema market, at the average film-goer. How would the Australian film critics respond?

When confronted with what turned out to be the most successful Australian film ever, the highest box-office earner in Australian history, the most successful foreign film ever released in the US, the only Australian film to be nominated for not one but three Academy Awards, would the nation's critics as a body recognize what they had been pining for all those years? In a word, no. Perhaps the sharpest criticism came from Phillip Adams, not only a respected columnist and advertising agency owner but head of the Australian Film Commission, the main sponsoring authority for the Australian film industry. For years Adams had been going to

Cannes along with some dogs of films and bewailing the fact that the Australian film industry was not making the sort of general-release breakthrough everyone was hoping and praying for. Adams saw a preview of *Crocodile Dundee* and was appalled. He thought it was terrible, and said so. Later in a long article in a newspaper, *The Australian*, he elaborated on why he thought, as the article's headline put it, 'Hoges – this time you've blown it'.

It seems slightly cruel to recall Adams's words – his selfless contribution to Australian films in particular and Australian culture in general is enormous – but they make the point of how wrong a lot of people were about *Crocodile Dundee* (Adams was also, alas, wrong about Paul's previous TV ad efforts). Hogan turned out to be a far better judge of a film than the critics were, at least those in Australia. Adams said it was his opinion that it was a mistake for Hogan to try to transfer his 'shrimp on the barbie' style to the big screen. 'Hogan will profoundly disappoint an increasingly impatient audience,' said Adams, adding: 'Throughout the film the pace is lifeless and Hogan's performance is lacklustre. . . . It's a film you yearn to take back to the editing bench to haul out half an hour. . . . Hoges damn near blows the entire film.' Adams went on to say, after criticizing the directing, the cinematography and the musical score, that the film ultimately failed (though he had no doubt it would be a great financial success) because it was confused about what it was trying to be: an adventure story or a comedy. 'If only Hogan had allowed XXXX (an unknown Australian comedy script writer) to go through the final draft and sharpen it up,' he added. Needless to say, XXXX, unlike the writers of *Crocodile Dundee*, has never been nominated for an Academy Award for script-writing and almost certainly never will be.

Several other Australian critics echoed Adams's condemnation. The *Bulletin*'s critic described *Crocodile Dundee*'s script as a 'ramshackle collection of whiskery jokes and well-loved clichés.' Had Hogan had a *good* script, the critic added, 'there's no telling what might happen' – words to come back and haunt a critic if ever there were! (This critic, however, saw the possibility that the film might be popular, Hogan having a certain undeniable charm.) Others were more perceptive. The *Sydney Morning Herald*'s Paul Byrnes recognized the film's worth: 'There is more wit in *Crocodile Dundee* than I can remember in any Australian movie of recent years.' He particularly liked the script; 'A lot of work has gone into refining it,' he said. 'It's tight and consistent.' And he enjoyed Hogan's performance: 'It deserves high praise.'

In the event, Australian film-goers proved to be more perceptive than the critics who carped and cavilled. As soon as the film opened in the capital cities, queues began to form at the ticket booths. Every performance was packed. It was, literally, an overnight sensation. By the end of the seventh week its takings had reached A$15.7 million and it was continuing to do over A$2 million of business each week. Meanwhile John Cornell flew over to California to negotiate foreign distribution rights. He sat around a swimming pool at his hotel and waited for the offers to come in. The phone rang loud and often. He struck a canny deal, selling North American rights – the main chance – to Paramount and rest-of-the-world rights to Twentieth Century Fox. A substantial proportion of what the film earned would go back to the original Australian syndicate that backed the film, and about half of this amount would go to Hogan and Cornell.

By the time the deal was done, *Crocodile Dundee* had become the biggest box-office success in Australian film history and had already recouped its production cost twice over. Paramount knew that they had a likely success on their hands with potential general appeal, so they decided to spend big bucks on pre-launch promotion. But first they wanted the film recut, refining some of the slang and cutting back the early Australian section. Then they worried about the title. It might be mistaken, they thought, for another animal film, like *Jaws* or *King Kong*. After reviewing 250 alternative titles they returned to the original one, adding a set of quotation marks around 'Crocodile' to avoid confusion. It was unusual for Paramount to 'pick up' a film not made in their own studios – they do it at most four or five times a year. They were going to be very glad they chose to pick up *Croc*. If Paul had been able to look into a crystal ball at this moment, just as *Crocodile Dundee* was poised to conquer the world, he would have seen more good fortune over the next couple of years than most people can expect in a lifetime. But something else he would have seen would have sent a shudder of fear through him. For he was about to be struck down in his prime.

CHAPTER 9

Struck Down

ON THE MORNING of Wednesday, 4 June 1986, Paul got into his car to drive down from his home at Belrose to his gym at Crows Nest, a suburb just across the bridge from the city on Sydney's north side. He'd been going to the gym regularly twice a week for the past few years. As he had told me when we met in London, he had felt middle-age approaching and wanted to try to keep fit. And as he drove into the heavier near-city traffic, he felt relaxed and super-fit.

He'd had three exhaustive medical check-ups in the past 18 months – one in New York, one at London's Harley Street, and a third in Sydney. It wasn't that he felt he needed these examinations. It had merely been to keep the insurance companies happy. With a ten million dollar cover on his life during the shooting of *Crocodile Dundee*, Paul's life was now worth much more than his weight in gold. In fact, Paul didn't weigh all that much. He'd never been physically big, and success had done little to put on the pounds. He was well under 11 stone, lean and muscular from years of workouts and weight lifting, not to mention his earlier exercise regime as a labourer and boxer. His blood pressure, the doctors had told him, was 110/75: that of a teenager. Not bad for a bloke of 45. Admittedly, he smoked quite a lot, and had the occasional tinny or two. But the doctors didn't seem to be bothered by this.

As he drove down the highway he smiled to himself (as he later told Sydney journalist Jerry Fetherston). Despite all the excitement of the success of *Crocodile Dundee* he'd taken it all in his stride. He told friends the only stress he'd felt lately was in working out how many millions he was making from the movie. Arriving at the gym, he started his warm-up exercises, then went on to do some bench press-ups. He was feeling a bit bored with the weights he'd been lifting lately, so he picked up the 91 kg one – almost one-third more than he weighed himself.

He'd been lifting that weight for a few weeks and had managed it without problems. But today, as he lifted the bar, he felt a sharp pain shoot through the back of his neck and head. His face suddenly felt deathly cold. Shaken, he at first thought he'd pinched a nerve in his neck. He tried to escape the pain by walking around for a while. But the jagged, searing sensation remained. So began what Paul was later to describe as 'the day my brain blew up'.

The pain continued to sharpen. A feeling of panic shot through him and he walked out of the gym and got into his car, started the engine and set off to drive the ten miles or so home. He began to feel nauseated and giddy. The pain was by now excruciating. He began vomiting. He caught sight of his face in the rear-vision mirror. His healthy tan had turned to a bright red flush. Barely able to see the road for the pain, Paul turned his car towards his doctor's home in the northern harbour suburb of Mosman. It must have been a hairy drive. But he finally got there. 'He took one look at me and knew instantly what was wrong,' Paul recalled later. 'He told me that he suspected a blood vessel had burst on the surface of the brain – a cerebral haemorrhage.' This rocked Hogan: 'I thought, "This can't be happening to me. This is some sort of crazy mistake." I've never even had a headache. I don't even get hangovers.'

After calling a neurologist, the doctor helped him to his car and drove him to the Royal North Shore Hospital at St Leonards, near Crows Nest. There the whisper soon swept the wards that Paul Hogan had been brought in and he was 'near death'. He was rushed to a private room where doctors started a series of tests to find out how much blood had escaped from the broken vessel into his brain. A painful spinal tap would help determine whether surgery would be necessary or not. Paul's wife Noelene had meanwhile arrived home from her shopping to find an urgent message to call Paul's doctor waiting for her. On hearing the terrible news, she drove as fast as she dared to the hospital and found her husband only semi-conscious and virtually unable to utter a word. Realizing how serious his condition was, she phoned John Cornell, who was at his home at Byron Bay, a beach resort far north of Sydney. He caught the first available plane and arrived at the hospital to join Noelene at Paul's bedside.

Cornell recalled finding Paul lying in a darkened room, his face contorted in agony. Cornell placed his hand on Paul's shoulder and said, 'This is a bit nasty, mate, interrupting our party.' Paul opened one eye and managed to speak. 'It will be a long party,' he whispered. Cornell booked himself into a motel close to the hospital and stayed near Paul during the coming days of agony and worry.

Another friend and co-star in *Crocodile*, John Meillon, said he didn't realize how serious Hogan's condition was until he was refused permission to see him. 'It seems he's a lot sicker than we first believed,' Meillon said after being turned away from the hospital. Occasionally Paul would open his eyes groggily. Sometimes he seemed to recognize his wife and best friend. Sometimes he didn't.

The doctors had decided not to operate. The best treatment, they believed, was to keep him sedated and try to ease the pain. He lay on his back, a saline drip feeding into a vein. The first bulletins on his condition released by the hospital played down the severity of his collapse. Doctors described his condition as 'satisfactory' but requiring 'complete bed rest and peace and quiet.' A hospital spokesperson said: 'The tests confirmed that Mr Hogan suffered a very small haemorrhage. A small amount of blood has escaped from a blood vessel on the surface of the brain. The haemorrhage has not left him with any disability but he still has a massive headache and is lying in a darkened room'.

A 'massive' headache proved to be an understatement. Paul's headache was gargantuan. The nurses were desperately pumping painkiller into him to try and stop the pain. He later described the agony as being 'like an eagle had its claws into my brain and was ripping it out.' On the third night he overheard a nurse saying that the staff didn't know what to do. Paul remembers overhearing one of the doctors saying to a colleague 'he's a goner unless we can get the blood pressure down.' He was beginning to suffer hallucinations. They were so bad, he said later, that they made the 'Exorcist' look like 'Snow White' by comparison to what he was experiencing.

Paul began to think he was going to die, and for a time, he felt resigned to it. But when a nurse asked him if he'd like to see a priest, a bit of the cheeky old Hoges came through. 'Not unless he's got a problem,' he quipped. The hallucinations were growing more vivid. Paul imagined his hospital room had started to flood. Water began trickling down the walls.

He saw women knitting people into an endless scarf. Yet he welcomed the hallucinations: 'I looked forward to them, they broke the monotony.' He tried to keep alert, wiggling his fingers and toes and counting up to 10 'to see if the brain was still functioning.' One day nurses found him huddled outside his room in the corridor, wearing a pair of fur boots a wellwisher had sent him.

Meanwhile, the whole of Australia and fans abroad in America and Britain were shocked by the news. Four thousand people, including Australian Prime Minister Bob Hawke, sent messages. So did the entire Australian Federal Parliament. The Tourism Minister, John Brown, told Parliament: 'I am sure every member of this House, recognizing the enormous contribution Paul Hogan, the Australian of the Year, has made to the tourism industry, will join me in wishing his return to full health is very speedy.' Brown's suggestion was acclaimed by both sides of the House, a rare moment of unity. Los Angeles Mayor Tom Bradley sent his get-well wishes. The Australian Tourist Commission regional director in Los Angeles, Alan Drew, said: 'I desperately hope he gets well soon. The man is a great Australian.' When Bob Hawke's gift of flowers was questioned by a newspaper, as being a rather 'sissy' thing for an Aussie bloke to send, Hawke's press secretary, Paul Ellercamp, snapped: 'Paul was feeling poorly. What was Hawke supposed to send? A crocodile?' Later, when Paul heard that Hawke was planning to visit him, he managed to quip that if the Prime Minister would promise NOT to visit him, he would promise to get better.

Thousands of ordinary well-wishers sent him gifts and cards, too. His room was packed with flowers. Cornell described the star of TV and film as 'lying in a garden of flowers'. In a brief moment of consciousness, Paul asked the nurses to distribute the flowers around all the wards of the hospital. When he was asked if he'd like a bigger room, he declined. 'Why would I need a bigger room?' he asked. Nevertheless, Cornell hired a bodyguard to stand at the door of the room to keep well-wishers at bay. Outside on the lawn opposite the hospital an army of Press, TV and radio reporters was encamped. Another contingent sat on the lawn of the Hogan family home. Already some papers had written Paul off – with kind words.

But by the second week of his ordeal a change had come over Paul. He found himself asking, 'What are they doing to Hoges?' And it seems that the Hoges aspect of his personality was what pulled him through. He began joking with the nurses – a sure sign of improvement. After 10 days on the saline drip, with no food, Paul slowly started to recover. He looked gaunt and exhausted, six kilos lighter than that almost-fatal day he had visited the gym. He asked why his kids – Brett, Clay, Todd, Lauren, and Scott – hadn't been in to visit him. Noelene told him that they *had* – every day. He hadn't been able to recognize them.

After two weeks he was discharged from hospital and advised by his doctors to take it easy but not to worry. 'They told me after the brain scan that it was a one-in-a-million thing and wasn't going to hurt me in the long run.' The doctors said he should try to forget it had ever happened to him. He was one of the lucky eight per cent of cerebral haemorrhage victims to survive with no after effects. It was highly unlikely that it would happen to him again. He should take Noelene away for a holiday. So they took off for Fiji. On his return Paul and Cornell held a Press conference at a Sydney hotel. A relieved Hogan, tanned again, but with deep lines still etched into his forehead, was introduced by John Cornell to the press conference as 'Paul Hogan, by special arrangement with God!'

'It's shaken my faith a bit,' Paul quipped to reporters. 'God must have nodded off there for a while, then woke up, looked down and said, "Ay, 'ang on, whatta you doin' to Hoges?" It was a million-to-one chance. Why it occurred nobody seems to know, although they reckon it didn't help for a skinny bloke like me to lift weights 23 kg (50 pounds) heavier than myself. I'm lucky it happened in a part of my brain I don't use. They said don't go around wearin' a crash helmet or change my lifestyle in any way. It won't happen again.'

Some people suggested he'd been under too much stress, but Paul dismissed any such idea: 'It wasn't stress,' he said. 'If I took it any easier I'd be a zombie. I'm really lazy. The hardest decision I ever had to make was whether to go out and mow the backyard or not. All those stories that blamed stress for what happened are crap.' Noelene echoed him: 'I've never known Paul to be stressed at all. He's always totally in command. People were saying he was run down and tired – he never gets tired. Probably the only time he's been stressed was on our wedding day.'

Throughout Paul's ordeal in hospital the calm, strong support of Noelene did much to help pull him through. Although she was extremely shocked and worried about his condition, she had set herself the task of trying not to reveal her fears to Paul or the family – although their five children knew her well enough to see the strain she was under. Some of the time she and the kids simply hadn't been able to believe what had happened. Paul had always been so fit and strong – indestructible. To see him collapsed in a screaming heap, as he later described his condition, was something they couldn't come to grips with.

During his hospitalization, Paul later learned, he had behaved in a very odd and bizarre manner. Suddenly he would rear up in bed and start shouting. 'Apparently I used to sit up and talk to the family, but all they were seeing was a different person, raving about things that didn't make sense,' he said. 'It was probably a bit hairy for them. I went crook at a couple of the grown-up kids once. I said, "Right, you're out of the will." I just couldn't remember them being there. I was right out of my head.'

Paul says he thinks his family must have felt a bit cheated when he collapsed. They'd never expected anything to happen to him. 'I guess I thought of myself as a cartoon character, like Popeye or Boofhead. They never got sick. I always carried on at home as if I was Superman, so when they suddenly realized that I wasn't, they all felt a little cheated.' He pays full tribute to Noelene for keeping her head in the crisis. 'I'll probably never know how hard it was for Noelene,' he said. 'She had to keep the kids' spirits up, keep the house running and cope with the press – something she hasn't had to handle before. She was absolutely terrific, she had to worry about me, and try to convince the kids I wasn't goin' to die.'

Gradually Paul began to feel better. Noelene prepared special meals to get those pounds back on her husband's almost skeletal frame. Gradually the lines of pain smoothed out and he began to be his old, laid-back self again. He was soon able to joke freely about the ordeal. It was reported that on one occasion he happened to bump into the medical writer from the *Sydney Morning Herald*, Chris Thomas, in the men's toilets at a North Shore restaurant. Thomas introduced himself as one of the reporters who had covered Paul's illness. 'I hope you weren't one of the blokes who said I was dead,' Paul replied. 'It was just a headache for me, but you blokes either had me with a massive stroke, dead or walking around like *this*', he continued, feigning paralysis to his left side. Jokes aside, he didn't forget his ordeal for a long time.

He spent a lot of his days wandering around his house, lazing beside his pool, recharging his batteries. Slowly the memory of the 'day his brain blew up' began to fade. But he would never again feel quite so secure about life: 'Until this happened I imagined myself appearing in films until I was 90. Now I think I'll turn it in when I'm 70.'

Two weeks after this quip, he jetted off to promote *Crocodile Dundee* around the United States, submitting to an exhausting programme of press, radio and TV interviews, day-in and day-out. Although he virtually said the same thing over and over again – Paul now has his life story off pat – he always delivered it with the inimitable Hogan charm and a flash of the Hogan smile. Few who saw him could tell that he had so recently escaped, not just from the film bite of a mechanical crocodile, but from the actual jaws of death.

CHAPTER 10

Croc of Gold

In the autumn of 1986 Hogan, Cornell and Linda Kozlowski went to New York for the September 26 premiere of their film. On the night it opened, you might have expected them to be sitting at a table at some exclusive Manhattan nightclub where champagne and caviar would be flowing lavishly. But they didn't follow the customary opening-night tradition at all. Instead, they drove around New York, dropping into cinemas here and there and standing in the back stalls, listening and observing the audiences' reactions. What they heard was music to their ears.

In New York the critics turned out to be more generous than some of their Australian counterparts. 'This is the stuff that myths are made of,' enthused the *New York Times* critic, comparing Mick Dundee with Paul Bunyan and Davy Crockett. 'Paul Hogan is delightful,' the critic added. 'He has an easy, extremely likeable screen personality – a mixture of warmth, sex-appeal, disarming innocence and dry humour.' The same critic found the script 'witty, with a fine sense of irony and the gift of poking fun at its own conceits.' (It may well have been this factor that so irked the film's

Australian critics.) And the critic added, 'Hogan has a wonderful deadpan forthrightness and humour.' Another critic raved, 'Australia, we owe you one. What can we give you, now that you've sent us Paul Hogan and *Crocodile Dundee? Crocodile Dundee* is wry, insightful, enjoyable and most of all funny. Hogan is perfect as Mick. A heart-throb without being slick, funny without being glib, a hero without being macho. *Crocodile Dundee* is a winner.'

Across America other critics agreed. 'He wins everyone over with his wit an charm,' effused the Los Angeles *Herald Examiner*. 'It's so wonderful to have a hero who is not using knives and violence and who you really like. Dundee is good, clean fun. Even the whores are nice people.' Audiences flocked to cinemas to see what a New Mexico movie-house owner called 'a film with cross-cultural appeal'. He added, 'Everyone's coming out for it – Indians, Hispanics and Anglos. *Crocodile Dundee* makes people feel good.' And another cinema owner said, 'It's almost beyond phenomenal.' Ads for the film said, 'Paul Hogan *is* Crocodile Dundee. There's a little of him in all of us.'

Moviegoers agreed. In its first seven weeks in the States *Croc* grossed over $50 million. By the start of the Christmas holiday season it had become the biggest autumn-release movie in history – foreign or American. Receipts rose to $70 million. By then it had passed the previous record for any foreign film, topping the revenues of *Chariots of Fire* and the various Bond movies. By mid-December it broke through the $100 million mark. By the end of the year it had surpassed all but one film – *Top Gun* – as the top movie earner of 1986, and *Croc* had been showing for only a fraction of the time *Top Gun* had been around. Well into 1987 it was still high in the audience ratings and a North American return of over $200 million seemed assured.

*　　　*　　　*

The reasons why the film turned out to be such an astonishing success are not easy to explain. Hogan himself had thought and hoped it would work, but never in their wildest dreams did he or Cornell imagine just *how* successful it would prove to be. 'I keep catching John's eye,' said Hogan, 'and we burst out laughing. We can't believe it.' There is no doubt that it was a film for its time. Even before its American premiere things Australian were all the rage in America (partly due to the success of Hogan's tourism advertisements). The America's Cup pre-publicity obviously had something to do with this, but it was more than that. America and perhaps the world needed something in late 1986, and Paul Hogan and *Crocodile Dundee* provided it.

One American academic, Reginald Foukes, Professor of English at the University of California at Los Angeles, said of Hogan: 'He's the noble savage of Spenser's *Faerie Queen* . . . or Orlando in Shakespeare's *As You Like It*, who triumphs over everybody and wins the girl. He appears to have nothing going for him and yet has everything going for him.' The head of Paramount, Frank Mancuso, put it another way: 'The surprising thing is that the appeal of the movie defies demographics and geography. It's bringing in the infrequent movie-goers, people who only go to the movies once or twice a year. It's bringing them in in every city across the country.'

The UK magazine *The Economist* tried to rationalize the Dundee phenomenon. 'Something out of the ordinary might be happening,' it said. 'The film's appeal may go deeper than its surface attractions. The screen's most recent winner-against-the-odds was a clunk called Rambo, who was not at all likeable. The innocent Australian who ambles and g'days through New York also comes out on top because he carries the bigger knife and knows how to use it. But he is empty of malice, unvengeful, and worries not a bit about standing tall. Could it be that Europe and America are attracted by that pre-Rambo thought about carrying a big stick and talking softly? Teddy Roosevelt would have enjoyed *Crocodile Dundee*.'

Hogan has his own explanation for his film's success. He thought one American critic had got it right. The critic said, 'I came out of the cinema feeling that you might just give the human race a second chance.' Hogan said, 'That's a terrific description. *Crocodile Dundee* makes people feel good, not just when they see the film but for a long time afterwards. People are even going back for a second helping. I just wish I could bottle that feeling and sell it.' Which is actually rather like what Hogan and Cornell did.

Certainly there isn't much doubt that the film struck a chord. The sex therapists Masters and Johnson recommended that male patients go to see *Crocodile Dundee* to learn how better to woo the ladies. All over America people were saying 'G'day' to each other. Tourists flocked to the Plaza Hotel in New York, where Mick Dundee stays in the film, and harassed the doorman, wanting to know more about the hotel's most famous guest. They wanted to know if Paul Hogan was still inside. Some wanted to put up for the night in the same room. The hotel's desk received a constant stream of complaints from guests demanding to know why *their* room didn't have a bidet as Mick Dundee's had in the film (he washed his smalls in it). The staff had to explain that that was typical Hogan artistic licence: the Plaza doesn't actually run to bidets in its rooms.

Whatever accounted for the appeal of Hogan and *Dundee*, it wasn't confined to America and Australia. When the film made its European debut just after Christmas 1986 it was another runaway success. In London, where it opened in

Leicester Square, it broke all opening-week box office records. So many people wanted to see the first performance that there was a mini-riot outside the cinema and police had to use loud-hailers to direct the crowds. In two months the film notched up more than $20 million in ticket sales in 296 cinemas throughout Britain. The eminent music critic and general pundit Bernard Levin raved about it in *The Times*, finding Hogan to be a mixture of Beowulf, King Arthur, Prince Charming, Robin Hood and Wagner's Parsifal. But not all UK critics were impressed. *The Spectator*'s Peter Ackroyd – a notorious hater of anything Australian – described the film as a case of 'mutton pumping iron like a lamb', ending his notice: 'Blah, blah, blah.' His review did, however, allow that Hogan had a gift of comic timing and a touch of English irony.

The film was a hit in Europe too. In France it outsold any other film local or foreign (and the French take their films more seriously than any other race on Earth). In the first three weeks of its release in West Germany more than three million cinema-goers saw what they called *Krokodil Dundee*. In Italy, where it was *Coccodrillo*, it also topped the ratings, as it did in several other countries. The interesting thing here was that there was no big promotional budget for drumming up ticket sales. The film's fame spread mainly by word of mouth. Whatever its alchemy was, frontiers or language barriers didn't stop it.

By now Paul Hogan was a superstar and rich beyond the dreams of avarice. At the age when most men are settling down to middle age and grandfatherhood, he had become an international sex symbol. In America there was something known as the 'Hogan distance'. It was about 10 feet and it was the distance Hogan could go in public without being recognized and mobbed by fans. It had been a long progress from the opal-mining town of Lightning Ridge via the Sydney Harbour Bridge to co-hosting the 1987 Hollywood Oscars ceremony – almost like a movie plot in itself. So where does Paul go from here? *Crocodile Dundee* will be a hard act to follow. Certainly he doesn't need the cash but already *Crocodile Dundee II* is on the way. He has said that if he couldn't make a sequel that was 'much, much better' than the first *Croc* movie, he wouldn't attempt it. The fact that he is making the second one bodes well.

And will Mick Dundee continue his career as a sex symbol? Will he start chasing pretty young girls? Paul grins and shakes his head at this kind of question. 'A young *woman*,' he says, 'and not too young. Mick is getting a bit too weatherbeaten for young girls.' He has also said that everybody wants the sequel set somewhere exotic – Paris or Beverly Hills. 'I'd like to see him in Japan.' But then he went on, 'I'm not greedy, I'm not hooked on adrenalin. I'm not craving public attention. I'm happy. At 31, I was a construction worker with no money and no prospects and no idea what I wanted to do. Six months later I had fame and fortune. If you're unhappy and miserable about that, then what do you want? You deserve to be struck by lightning.'

All the success still hasn't gone to Paul's head. Certainly he will not be doing a sequel primarily for the money. He once told one British reporter, 'I've never had any desire for yachts or actresses or fast horses. I've got the ultimate job, making people laugh and getting paid for it, and I wouldn't swap places with anyone. I don't wanna be a prime minister or a brain surgeon. I don't do it for the money, y'know. All you need is enough to tell 'em to get stuffed.' The sequel is being kept under very tight wraps. But Paul did suggest that more of the story would be set in America this time.

The timing of Paul's show-business career, unlike his earlier bumbling from one labouring job to the next, has a neat pattern to it, at least in retrospect. With the guiding genius of Cornell, coupled with Paul's own natural pacing, he doesn't appear to have put a foot wrong. Although *Crocodile Dundee* was chosen for only a minor Oscar nomination – for Best Screenplay – the choice of Paul to help host the Oscars was a popular one and his performance on the night won him even more friends around the world. Next time around, he'd be in an ideal position for the main award. Cornell summed up his feelings about being Paul's manager, revealing how this 'pacing' of Paul's career occurred: 'There's no greed in him. He is street-smart, a touch shy. He can be a bit lazy but I don't think the mind stops often. One of my jobs is to prod him a bit. I wanted him to abandon television after 60 or 70 shows. I was prodding him to do a film but I knew it would have to come out of his head.'

Paul is a superstar now, but he still doesn't 'put on the dog', preferring to enjoy a quiet domestic life at home in Sydney. 'I'm like everyone else at home: I get cut off in mid-sentence when I'm talking, so you can't be a star at home.' He added, 'I'm not the star in my home (which he has described as 'The Greta Garbo Home for Wayward Boys and Girls'). With a house full of kids you come home at the end of the day and you're ready to tell them what wonderful things you've done, and they say, "Shut up, Dad, we're watching *Gilligan's Island*" or whatever on TV. They keep things in perspective. The house we've got is just a big, friendly lunatic asylum. I've got all my kids there – and their wives, girlfriends or boyfriends – and dinner at home is somewhere between six and 14 people. It's a noisy house . . . a lot of friendly fighting and yelling, and a lot of music.' His teenage daughter, Lauren, grabs his most passionate fan letters and reads them with glee, exclaiming, 'Listen to this one, Dad!' and roaring with laughter.

Asked if his lifestyle had changed greatly since he started

making money, he says, 'I reckon I'm probably eating better than I was when I was on the Harbour Bridge.' This relaxed normality is echoed in his attitude to clothes and other possessions, like cars. He dresses simply in sportswear, bought by Noelene, and certainly wouldn't think of wearing any male jewellery, shaking his head at the idea of 'having chains hangin' round me neck'. His main sartorial advice is: 'Never wear socks with thongs' (flipflops), and 'Never polish your shoes, that'd make the rest of your clothes look even scruffier.' Paul didn't even get round to buying a flashy car until recently, and that was only after a puzzled journalist had asked him, 'Don't you have any toys?' and Noelene had said, 'Go and buy yourself a nice, nifty car.' So Paul had gone down to a car showroom full of Maseratis and Ferraris, and ended up buying a Porsche – because it was 'the closest thing to a motorbike.'

Especially now he is world-famous, Cornell guards Paul closely, preventing him from being photographed in his Porsche or from appearing on shows that concentrate on the lifestyles of the rich and famous. The common touch must be preserved at all cost. A nice little story on this theme is related in the American magazine *Newsweek* about the time Cornell saw Paul reaching to pick up a James Bond paperback. Cornell jumped up from his chair and said, 'Don't start reading bloody books. You're liable to become literate and ruin the whole thing!'

Although he is more protected now from the press, Paul still has a sensible approach to being a celebrity, happily signing autographs when he's in public: 'I've always figured that if you want your privacy, you sing in the shower, you don't get up on the bloody stage.' But as his fame grows, he is becoming concerned that people are starting to take too much notice of his every word. At the press conference when he came out of hospital after his cerebral haemhorrage, he let slip an aside about Prime Minister Hawke being out of touch with the populace. He was abashed when next day Hawke felt he had to go on TV to refute 'the charges'. 'I have no political ambitions,' Paul said.

Or has he? A few years ago he put on a TV special called 'Paul Hogan for Prime Minister' in which he presented a mock campaign for the top job in Australia, coming out with the statement that he would actually like to be Australia's leader. So taken with this idea was his audience that in the following real General Election more than 70,000 Australian voters wrote in his name on their ballot papers.

Paul has always maintained that he has no real desire to become a politician, despite the success other show business personalities have had in this field. Yet more than once he has let drop some rather political statements. More than once he has said, for example, that if he was in charge of Australia he would turn it into a benign dictatorship with himself at its head, adding that he would order only the occasional beheading. On another occasion he said, 'I like the good old-fashioned politician who lies. I like the good old days when we got promised all sorts of heavens. No tax. Things would be prosperous. Everyone would have jobs. In those days we knew all the promises that politicians made were lies, so we did not hold them to them. But it was a cheerful time.'

Paul likes to make out that he is essentially a simple person, a happy-go-lucky comic. He says, 'My ancestors were the guys with the bells on their hats – and I miss the freedom that I had for so many years as a simple clown.' This is yet another reason why he continues to cherish the privacy of his own home and doesn't do what so many stars do, professing to be a 'very private person' and at the same moment allowing magazines to photograph him in his 'private, secret hideaway.' 'I don't have the trappings of a millionaire but I'm not a closet leftwinger either,' he explained. 'If I needed a car to drive regularly I'd probably have a Rolls-Royce and a chauffeur. I stay in five-star hotels and I travel first class. And these days I get up when I wake up. As Johnny Speight (the English writer who invented the character Alf Garnett) says, all you want out of life is enough money to say no: no, I don't want to do an unfunny film. No, I don't have to appear on a television show I don't like.'

Nor does Paul want to live in Hollywood, despite plenty of enticements from the big movie companies for him to do so. Unlike many of Australia's other stars, celebrities and sporting personalities, such as Olivia Newton John, tennis players Evonne Goolagong-Cawley and Lew Hoad, film producers Bruce Beresford and Fred Schepisi, or publishing tycoon Rupert Murdoch, Paul sees no reason to stop living in Australia, the country he loves. Despite constant rumours that he has forked out millions on a Bel Air mansion, Paul says he'll stick to Oz. 'I'd look a bit of a pelican inviting you Americans to my country when I was living in your country,' he told Cable News Network TV's interviewer Larry King in 1986. On the other hand, he does plan to spend time outside Australia, making movies, in America, England, Spain, Japan – wherever may be the right place to film a specific project.

Cornell agrees with Paul that the future now lies in movies: 'I think we're in the movie game now,' he said in March 1986. 'We'll have a shot at two or three movies in the next five or six years. Movies are like drilling oil wells, you know – if you hit a good one you can get a huge reward. To stay at home and say "I'll only make Australian films" is to limit yourself a bit.' He made these comments just before *Crocodile Dundee* took off in the States. And he also stood up for the directors who have left Australia. 'Some people bag them for that. But they're directors! That's what they do. They don't want to sit at home and every three years do a low-budget art film. So, what are they meant to do in between? Work for the Department of Main Roads? Anyway, if they all stayed home, with the small industry we've got, there'd be no new directors. The big names would be directing all the films that came out of Australia.'

It will be fascinating to see what Paul Hogan achieves over the coming years. His success is due not so much to luck as to destiny. Back in the days when he laired* around Sydney's western suburbs, doing handstands on his motorbike, impressing the birds with his acrobatic diving down at the Granville Baths, mucking about with his mates on the Coathanger – it was all part of Paul's need to express himself, to perform. He says he never had a specific desire for a career in show-business. But he had always felt he had an ability to do something: 'I thought I'd do something different, I didn't know what. But you sort of know sometimes that you march to the beat of a different drummer. I was a bit of a fatalist. I did have the feeling that something will come along that will suit me. You start to wonder when you're 30 when it's coming. But the thing is to stick your nose in the door when it opens and have a go. And then don't sit there.' On another occasion, back in 1981, he admitted he liked money: 'I'm into money. But I'm not into little amounts of money. I'm into big amounts of money.' Prophetic words, indeed.

Looking back on what made his success, he says ' 'aving a go, that's what made me. Then a lotta luck. But you've gotta make the first move yourself.' He said that when he first bobbed up on *New Faces* back in 1972, 'that was 90 per cent Hoges, getting up people, giving a bit of cheek, not giving a damn – without much motive or thought behind it. But 10 per cent of me knew what I was doing. After a while you realize it's no longer just a joke but something that can sustain a career. You grow up a bit. If I'd stayed Hoges, I'd be down the pub now, shouting the bar, back with the chook* raffles.'

Like most people who have met him, I found the real Paul Hogan to be a much quieter, more complex person than he appears on screen. You get the feeling that behind that laconic manner and the terse sentences lies a highly intelligent and sensitive person. 'He's a quiet, private, rather awkward fellow,' says Jane Scott, line producer on *Crocodile Dundee*. But he rarely lets down his guard: that's typically Australian. Nobody likes to show too much sentiment and nobody likes a smart alec who's too clever by half. Perhaps the most telling thing about Paul Hogan's success is that despite coming from a nation that is notorious for 'cutting down its tall poppies'* – scything down to size anyone who becomes famous or important – he has survived so far. He once said he wasn't a poppy, he was 'an ironbark tree'. He is still liked by most of his fellow Australians, who say, 'Good on yer, mate. You've done us proud.'

GLOSSARY

Lingo

Paul Hogan's mother tongue, as some of his American fans were surprised to learn, is English – but strictly speaking, it's a distinct dialect called Australian English, which is unique to the Great Southern Continent yet has affinities to other far-flung tongues, particularly New Zealand English. Hogan's Australian lingo is one of two indigenous sub-dialects, broad and educated, the former being his natural or mother tongue. Educated Australian, on the other hand, is an antipodean attempt to mimic standard (or BBC or Home Counties) English and used to be what Australian children were taught at school by parents anxious to ensure their offspring talked 'proper' so they would not appear to be colonial half-wits.

Lately a movement called Australian nationalism (also known as ockerism), which itself is a product of disengagement from the Old Country, has led to a decline in the use and popularity of educated Australian. Indeed, now it's considered almost *de rigueur* in many Down Under circles to talk ostentatiously in broad Australian – the broader the better – and even Prime Ministers drag out their vowels and resonate their nasal passages so they can appear to the discerning voter just as plain and simple as Hogan or any other dinki-di, fair dinkum Aussie.

Hogan is to this curious renaissance, this golden age of 'a's that sound like 'i's, as Babe Ruth was to American baseball fans or Dennis Connor is to America's Cup racing; in other words, he's a champion, even a prophet. He is, in his way, the Shakespeare, or at least the Damon Runyon, of his time and place.

Keen observers will note that when Hogan speaks he does not place too much of a burden on his lips. They hardly move. This is one of the main characteristics of broad Australian and is traceable, say the experts, to the inordinate number of flies that pervade the Australian continent. Even before the white man came, flies were a problem, which is why the aborigines also say as little as possible. You will not go far anywhere in Australia, particularly outdoors in warmer weather, without discovering that you are in the company of swarms of flies. Mostly they are of the small variety and are known as bush flies. They alight on one's person like cruise passengers joining a liner. This phenomenon is the origin of what is called The Great Australian Salute, which is a kind of repetitive swatting motion of the hand and arm and is ubiquitous across the continent, though more prevalent in rural regions. The same phenomenon, incidentally, also explains why the accent is broader the further you get away from towns. (Cattle do the Salute with their tails.)

Visitors may also observe another curious national habit: many Australians carry their own personal spray cans and every now and again spray their hands and face (and legs, if exposed) with fly repellent. This item of modern technology, by the way, replaces the more traditional protective screen: a hat with corks dangling from the brim.

Early colonists soon discovered that even with the aid of

corks and The Great Australian Salute, any form of speech involving appreciable lip and mouth activity, as the English of the Old Country did, permitted the ingress of flies to the facial cavity. Thus, over almost two centuries now, it has become the habit of Australians to speak as little as possible, and then only with the mouth minimally open, as if one were practising ventriloquy. Thus broad Australian, Hogan's natural language, developed. Indeed, today in a room crowded with Australians it is often hard to tell from whose mouth the talk is emitting (NB: 'to throw your voice', however, is to regurgitate).

Hoges's mode of communication has other peculiarities, too. One is a tendency, evinced by all true Aussies, to run their words together. Often entire sentences are uttered as if they were a single noun or verb. 'G'day', Hoges's catch-phrase, is a simple example. 'Havagooday' is another common one. 'Howyagoinmate' is another. This technique is designed to deliver the maximum amount of verbal information in the shortest space of time, giving the flies minimum opportunity to effect an entry. A typical exchange between two Australians meeting each other outdoors at the height of the fly season might (and often does) go thus:

> 1st Aussie: 'Waddayaknow?'
> 2nd Aussie: 'Noddalot.'

End of conversation.

Another oddity is the tendency to abbreviate, for reasons that will now be obvious. Simple Australian nouns almost always end in either 'o' or 'ie'. Aborigines are abos; aggravation is aggro; ammunition is ammo; afternoon is arvo; compensation is compo; a journalist is a journo; a garbo is a garbage collector, etc., etc. The 'ie' mode can be illustrated in the following short Australian story:

Bluey, a cabbie, took a sickie. He was up Rockie
(Rockhampton, a Queenie town) on hollies seeing
some rellies. He had brekkie listening to his trannie
and reading the Tele (the Telegraph, a newspaper).
His brickie mate, Lofty, was away in Tassie
(Tasmania, an Aussie State) with a (air) hostie, or he
would have asked him round to drink a frostie.
He backed out the Volksie, did a wheelie (or a uey),
nearly ran down the postie, who gave him a few
roughies (see glossary) which he put on with his
bookie, then went out and did his winnings on the
pokies.

It will also be noted that most Australians, particularly
the male variety (and it's odd that most Australian slang is
male-oriented), have strange names. No real Aussie can be
safely left with the monicker he or she was first endowed
with. Barry is Bazza, Charles is Chilla; John is Johnno;
Shirley is Shirl; Bruce is Brucie (it's a belief held widely in
Britain that all Australians are called Brucie); Douglas is
Duggie; and so on. If by chance a first name isn't readily
amenable to such diminutization, then they attack the
surname. Thus Paul Hogan is always called Hoges in
Australia. (Incidentally, all red-headed people are called
Bluey, short people Lofty, and similar. This is what some
experts call the Australian sense of humour.)

Professors who know about such things say that Hoges's
Australian is distinctive for its nasal twang and short vowels
(it does not, however, have the glottal stop of London
cockney, with which it is often confused). So remarkable is
the Aussie twang that a term has been invented for it: Strine,
which is short for Australian (if you say it quickly enough
and push it through your nose it sounds like 'strine'). One
Australian expert has codified this twang, described by one

visitor as 'sounding like a wild duck singing Annie Laurie under water', into a sub-language with its own grammar and vocabulary. For example, if you hear Hoges or any other Aussie say 'trine', you will now know he's referring to the train. The 'tan cancel' is the town council. And what in Australia is a 'tea nature' is elsewhere a 'teenager'.

Another interesting feature of the language Hogan speaks is the richness of its imagery. It is replete with colourful turns of phrase, regrettably many either scatological or to do with sex or booze. When Hoges speaks, for example, of 'bunging on more side than a rat with gold teeth' he is, of course, referring to someone showing off. Naturally 'meals on wheels' are girls and 'flat out like a lizard drinking' implies sleep. Someone who 'wouldn't shout in a shark attack' is a mean or stingy person. Much of his vocabulary will be familiar already (a tinny is quite clearly a can of beer and a barbie is a barbecue). But others will be a trifle obscure and as he becomes, as he undoubtedly is destined to be, more of an international figure and Australian culture in general impinges on the wider world, then some help will be needed initially to fully appreciate the subtleties of this marvellous instrument, the Australian language. To assist understanding, here is a glossary of some of the more common or more difficult Australianisms:

<h1 style="text-align:center">B</h1>

Back o' Bourke: remote from civilization (see **black stump**)
Barbie: barbecue ('Put another shrimp – or prawn – on the barbie')

Bite: to borrow money (see also **fang**)
Bitumen blonde: an aboriginal lady
Black stump, beyond the: further even than Bourke
Black velvet: an aboriginal girl
Block, to do one's: lose one's temper
Bludge: cadge, exploit ('a bloody dole-bludger')
Bonzer: good
Boong: a coloured individual
Bottler: a very good person ('He's a bloody bottler')
Bullamakanka: somewhere in the **bush** (see **woop-woop**)
Burl: an attempt ('Give it a burl, mate')

C

Cackleberries: eggs
Chiack: indulge in banter (pronounced 'shy-ak')
Chilla: The Heir to the (UK) Throne, or other individual
    named Charles
Chloe, drunk as: very inebriated
Chook: a fowl ('May all yer chooks turn into emus and
    kick yer dunny down' – a popular antipodean curse)
Chromo: prostitute, possibly also a lesbian
Coathanger, the: Sydney Harbour Bridge
Coo-ee: a call in the bush (archaic)
Crash hot: rather good (polite for **shit hot**)
Crook: ill

D

Dag: a very silly or funny individual

Derro: city tramp (**metho:** a derro who drinks
    methalated spirits)
Dinki-di: genuine (archaic) ('He's a dinki-di Aussie')
Divvy: share out
Dob in: tell on or betray

E

Esky: an insulated receptacle for transporting beer

F

Fang: to borrow money ('I fanged him for a fiver')
Fish, the: name of a train
Floater: a south Australian delicacy (actually a pie with
    peas)
Flynn, in like: sexual success (after the famous
    Australian actor)
Furphy: an untrue story

G

Galah: dope, dill, drongo, *i.e.* stupid person
Garbo: sanitary engineer, *i.e.* garbage collector or
    dustman
Gin: aboriginal lady (archaic)
Goanna: Australian lizard, prized as aborigines' snack
    ('I'm so hungry I could eat a goanna between two
    slabs of bark')
Goog, full as a: drunk

H

Hardy, crack to: be philosophical, make light of
Hoo-roo: Goodbye (alternatively, a call for attention)
Hide: cheek ('What a hide!')
Hughie: the Deity; a *deus ex machina* ('Send it down, Hughie')
Hump the bluey: to go **walkabout** carrying a **swag**
Humpy: a small hut or shack

I

Iceberg: out-of-season swimmer
Ikey-mo: Jewish person (Mo: a famous Hebrew comic in Sydney)

J

Jackaroo: a trainee working on a country property; a dude (fem. **Jillaroo**)
Jack of, to be: be tired of or be rid of
Jack up: to refuse
Jacky: affectionate term for male aborigine
Jake: fine, OK ('She's jake, mate')
Jam: affected accent or airs (as in 'putting on the jam')
Job: to punch ('Say that again and I'll job you')

K

Kick in: to pay one's share

L

Lair: show-off
Larrikin: street-smart youth
Lucky Country, the: Oz
Lurk, a: sinecure or dodge of some kind

M

Market, to go to: become very angry
Molly-dooker: a left-handed person (also: **kacky-
    hander**)
Moral: a sure thing, a certainty

N

Nark: spoil-sport, even a **wowser** (see below)
Nasho: National Service, Australia's peace-time military
    draft
Ning-nong: dope, dill, drongo, i.e. stupid person
Norks: knockers

O

Ocker: a red-necked Aussie; anything overtly Australian
Out to it: drunk, spiflicated, paralytic, shickered (see
    below)
Over the fence: too much, unreasonable

P

Pack, to go to the: collapse, disintegrate
Park, to: regurgitate ('Where did you park the tiger?')
Pea: a certainty (also: shoo-in)
Perve: appreciate sexually ('Get a perve at those sheilas')
Pie-eater: an ordinary or simple person
Poke borak at: deride; insult
Pongo: an English person, allegedly scatological
Possie: a position or mild **lurk** ('Get a good possie, Bert')
Push: a gang (archaic)

Q

Quandong: a female who fails to feature after wining and
  dining
Quid: (archaic) pound sterling, as in 'not the full quid'

R

Rafferty rules: anything goes; free for all
Razoo: a small coin ('I haven't a brass razoo')
Rockhopper: a seaside fisherman
Rooted: plumb tuckered out
Rort: a dodge or trick ('Peace and sports, not war and
  rorts')
Rotten: fairly inebriated ('He was rotten')
Roughie: a long-shot at the races
RSL, the: a club where **Diggers** (see above) and other
  Australians congregate (Returned Servicemen's
  League)
Rudie: a semantic solecism or swear word

S

Shag on a rock: something abandoned ('I was left like a
    shag on a rock')
Shickered: drunk
Shivoo: a party or **beano**; social occasion
Sickie: a day off
Skite: to boast
Skivvy: a loose shirt
Sky pilot: clergyman
Smoko: a period of R&R (rest and recreation)
Smooge: to be affectionate
Snowdropper: a thief who preys on washing hung out to
    dry
Sparrow fart: dawn
Spine basher: a loafer
Stir the possum: promote dissension; cause trouble
Stonkered: drunk (yet again, alas)
Stubbies: glass receptacles for beer; a pair of shorts
Swaggie: a country tramp

T

Tall poppy: anyone important, normally a term of
    contempt
Two-up: an illegal gambling game (also swy)
Tyke: a mick, a person of the Roman Catholic persuasion

U

Underground mutton: rabbit
Urger: trickster or con-man

W

Wallopers: the constabulary; boys in blue; police
Whacko-the-diddle-o: jubilation
White ant: undermine or sabotage
Wingding: a **beano** (see **Shivoo**)
Woop-woop: a long way away; alt. for **bullamakanka**
    (see above)
Wowser: narrow-minded, intolerant person

Y

Yabba: talk
Yakka: work